THE IDEOLOGY
of
BLACKNESS

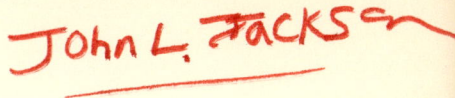

THE IDEOLOGY
of
BLACKNESS

Edited and with an
Introduction by
RAYMOND F. BETTS
GRINNELL COLLEGE

D. C. HEATH AND COMPANY
Lexington, Massachusetts

Copyright © 1971 by D.C. Heath and Company.

All rights reserved. No part of this publication may be reproduced or transmitted in any form or by any means, electronic or mechanical, including photocopy, recording, or any information storage or retrieval system, without permission in writing from the publisher.

Published simultaneously in Canada.

Printed in the United States of America.

Library of Congress Catalog Card Number: 72-145699

Preface

The history of Africa in the modern world is charged with drama and wracked with suffering. Undergoing a diaspora more tragic than that endured by the Jewish people, the Africans were forced, with the advent of the slave trade, into the most widespread involuntary migration the world has known. They were also forced to assume the habits and social patterns of the alien cultures into which they were intruded. Those many more who remained in Africa underwent a much less severe but still disorienting experience when European imperialism spread over the continent at the end of the nineteenth century.

Everywhere he found himself, the black was thus placed in a psychologically disturbing and socially oppressive system. He was told that he had no past, at least no past worth recording; he was told that his future depended upon his ability to imitate the very peoples who had enslaved him. In reaction to such condescending assertions, the radical black intellectual began to respond ideologically. Ideology is here used in a cultural sense, to denote the verbal iconography by which a people represents itself in order to achieve communal purpose.

The attempt to define a culture and a social order which issued from and would respond to the needs of black people was the intellectual concern of the persons whose works have been excerpted in this anthology. Editorial attention has therefore been centered on those assessments of the historical, literary, and—most obviously—cultural characteristics that authors have considered to be the distinctive qualities of the black experience and ethos. Particular political strategies and policies, ranging from the American civil rights movement to the Pan-African movement, do not therefore figure in this anthology.

As the cultural phenomenon here being considered is of tricontinental proportions, an effort has been made to select works that suggest the commonalty of themes, most of which revolve about a particular life-style that is believed either to inhere in the black or

PREFACE

to be traditionally derived from a precolonial past or to be emergent from the constraints of white racism.

The editor would argue that while intimate familiarity with the sense and meaning of this ideology may be available only to the black himself, knowledge and appreciation of the ideology can and ought to be grasped by anyone who would openly try. It is hoped that the anthology will serve this particular purpose.

R.F.B.

Contents

INTRODUCTION
1

PART I

THE FORMATIVE PERIOD
Toward Cultural Definition

MARTIN ROBINSON DELANY

Selections from *The Condition, Elevation, Emigration, and Destiny of the Colored People of the United States*
21

EDWARD WILMOT BLYDEN

Selections from *Christianity, Islam, and the Negro Race*
25

MOJOLA AGBEBI

Selections from *Inaugural Sermon*
43

WILLIAM EDWARD BURGHARDT DU BOIS

Selection from *The Souls of Black Folk*
47

J. E. CASELY HAYFORD

Selections from *Ethiopia Unbound: Studies in Race Emancipation*
55

CONTENTS

MARCUS AURELIUS GARVEY

Selections from *Philosophy and Opinions of Marcus Garvey*
63

PART II

CULTURAL RENAISSANCE
Black Aesthetics and Life-Style

COUNTEE CULLEN

Heritage
75

LANGSTON HUGHES

The Negro Artist and the Racial Mountain
81

JEAN PRICE-MARS

Selections from *Ainsi parla l'oncle*
87

LOUIS-THOMAS ACHILLE

Art and the Blacks
95

AIMÉ CÉSAIRE

Selections from *Cahier d'un retour au pays natal*
103

LÉOPOLD SÉDAR SENGHOR

Black Woman
107

African-Negro Aesthetics
110

CONTENTS

CHEIKH ANTA DIOP

Selections from *Nations nègres et culture*
127

SAMUEL W. ALLEN

Selections from *Negritude and Its Relevance for the American Negro Writer*
135

PART III

REAPPRAISAL OF THE BLACK CULTURAL EXPERIENCE IN AMERICA

HAROLD WRIGHT CRUSE

Selections from *An Afro-American's Cultural Views*
149

MALCOLM X

Selections from *Malcolm X Speaks*
157

LEROI JONES

Selections from *The Legacy of Malcolm X, and the Coming of the Black Nation*
161

PART IV

RECENT CRITICISMS AND NEW DIRECTIONS

FRANTZ FANON

Selections from *The Wretched of the Earth*
169

CONTENTS

EZEKIEL MPHAHLELE

A Reply
177

STANISLAS ADOTEVI

Selections from The Strategy of Culture
185

MARTIN L. KILSON, JR.

The Intellectual Validity of Studying the Black Experience
197

ERNIE MKALIMOTO

Revolutionary Black Culture:
The Cultural Arm of Revolutionary Nationalism
201

Annotated Bibliography
211

Introduction

The ideology of blackness is an expression of protest and affirmation, arising searingly from the souls of men who have been denied human dignity and who now claim their own future. Variously voiced on several continents where the black man has been visited with white sociopolitical domination, this ideology is multiform in expression, ranging from rhapsodic poem to bitter polemic, and from political speech to academic tract. As it has traversed time in its development, it has become more forcefully articulated and militantly asserted, reaching its highest degree of popularity, influence, and elaboration in our own era.

Along with its impressive historical dimensions, the ideology of blackness exhibits considerable coherence, not so much in well-defined doctrine or well-developed system, as in ideals and values, images and rhetoric, joined with the thought of forming a cultural matrix for a new black society. Thus, the ideology of blackness is essentially a cultural phenomenon for which the descriptive word "style" serves as an appropriate analogue for the strategic word "soul."

Manifested wherever the black experience has occurred, the ideology necessarily places in opposition the white and black worlds. In great part it is a calculated reversal of values and an overturning of old myths. Behind the appealing epigram "Black is beautiful" is found denunciation of white-determined values and white-structured institutions that have demeaned and shackled the black. Beyond the epigram is the far-reaching desire to create a new organic community which will be proud and vibrant. The attempt to define a black aesthetic based on the black experience, to find a particular black idiom both for artistic and political purposes, and to reform historical interpretation so that the black will be liberated from the subordinate position assigned him in most Western historical accounts—these are all aspects of the search or research for collective identity and, derivatively, for distinctive personality.

INTRODUCTION

No doubt the most forceful and telling statements posited to date by black cultural ideologues, regardless of geographical location, have been of a negative sort: denunciations of racism, colonialism, and Westernization. All of the traditional intellectual baggage of modern Western civilization, bearing the labels of liberalism, democracy, and individualism, has been searched and frequently cast aside. And so occasionally have the prevalent theories of unilinear social development supposedly guided by a white center line, theories often euphemized in terms like "progress" and "modernization."

In place of the chaotic and fragmented West created and inhabited by the white man, the radical philosophical advocates of blackness would offer a new cultural unity, one that is communal and harmonious. The dualism of Western reality—the mind-and-body problem—is here to be resolved by affirmation of an existential wholeness, the belief in universal perception and total participation through feeling and being, the empathetic involvement with the world all about, as against antagonistic detachment from it. Spontaneity and laughter, spirituality and soulfulness, rhythm and movement—these all have been frequently listed as qualities indicating the cohesiveness and pleasing dimensions of the black world.

A historical perspective on this world has also been considered of great importance. In much of the writing on blackness the theme of the African heritage has been stressed, with some authors extending their search backward to Pharaonic Egypt, which they argue was essentially a black civilization. Moreover, some comparisons have been made between precolonial Africa and the West, with the former seen as yielding a cooperative and pacific way of communal life, the latter an aggressive and competitive one.

This brief recapitulation of some of the frequently presented characteristics of the condition of blackness suggests that this ideology, like others, is chiefly defined in terms of contrast, contrast in this particular instance with the dominant values and structures of the established—or recently disestablished—order. More particularly, the ideology of blackness was born of the "colonial situation," that domination and suppression of blacks by whites, whether achieved by an alien white minority in tropical Africa or by a residential white majority surrounding and repressing an American black ghetto. In defiance of this situation, the ideology of blackness can be viewed as an assertion of ethnic identity and pride. In most extended form it becomes cultural nationalism, both defensive and regenerative, postulated upon the observation that social destruction is conditioned by cultural destruction and, conversely, that social cohesion can be achieved only by cultural unity. The historical location of this observation is easily found.

The inescapable condition of the black man in the white-oriented world was, obviously, his color. In both the American and the colonial African situation, pigmented politics prevailed: segregation, color-bar, and apartheid are tragic expressions of this. As a minor biological factor was made an essential social condition, the black was forced into a lowly state where he was exploited and contemptuously dismissed as something less than human. Prevailing liberal ideas that opposed this treatment were directed to universal homogenization—the "melting pot" theme—in which only the individual and the global society were made to count. Both traditional colonial assimilation and American integration were based on a unidirectional cultural attainment: "be like us" was the imperative of this social philosophy, of which the necessary complement was "deny yourself."

The result of this social conditioning was individually disturbing. In sensitive and reflective writers like the Martiniquan Frantz Fanon, who spoke of "the zebra striping of my mind," it created a person who was culturally ambivalent, neither black nor white, uprooted from one way of life and denied full entry into the other.[1] Thus situated, some black intellectuals assumed that there was only one means of viable social and cultural escape: self-identification through ethnic revolt. The ideology of blackness was that ideology of revolt, manifesting itself in terms of romantic literature dedicated to an idealized black type and black past, defining itself in terms of philosophical assessments of the black experience, and searching for that metaphysical quality which W. E. B. Du Bois has called "the soul-beauty of a race."

To appreciate the differences and nuances exhibited by this literature, one is obliged to trace its various historical strands.

Extending back over a hundred years, the ideology of blackness has also extended over continents. This traffic in ideas was transatlantic, indicating a cultural commerce derived from similar responses to racial oppression and similar appreciations of the need for new communal definitions. In retrospect, one can discern two triangular patterns, representing two different periods and moods: The first joined the United States, the Caribbean Islands, and West Africa, and extended from the late nineteenth century into the early twentieth century; the second joined the Caribbean, Harlem, and

---

[1] On this subject see the sensitive and very perceptive analysis offered by Frantz Fanon in his *Black Skin, White Masks* (New York: Grove Press, 1967).

INTRODUCTION

Paris, and extended through four intensive decades, the 1920's to the 1950's.[2]

The formative period of ideological development exhibited nothing approaching a well-defined school or grouping of authors. Those blacks who turned their attention to the subject of their ethnic condition and experience were scattered, but joined in common purpose: to appraise their present subordinate position and to determine modes of thought and means of action to alleviate it. This was the initial period of racial awakening and solidarity; it witnessed the beginning of the "Back-to-Africa" movement, which would reach its culmination in the work and thought of Marcus Garvey; it witnessed the first search by blacks for a past denied them by white European and American; it witnessed the emergence of a black press, ranging in region of publication from the West Coast of Africa to the East Coast of the United States.

The impressive number of black writers who raised their voices in protest and hope at this time included well-known figures like the Americans Frederick Douglass and Bishop H. M. Turner of the African Methodist Episcopal Church; and the African clerics Bishop Samuel Crowther and Bishop James Johnson. But perhaps the first of this number to articulate a point of view and to present a perspective that might be called formative of the ideology of blackness was the American Martin Robinson Delany, one-time journalist, Harvard medical student, Union Army Major, and explorer of the Niger. His *The Condition, Elevation, Emigration, and Destiny of the Colored People of the United States,* published in 1852, was a seminal work in the history of writings on the black ethos. Reviewing the social condition and achievements of blacks in the United States, he urged his race to prepare its own destiny, to assume a new role and a new position in world affairs.[3]

> The time has now fully arrived, when the colored race is called upon by all the ties of common humanity, and all the claims of consummate justice, to go forward and take their position, and do battle in the struggle now being made for the redemption of the world. . . . Our race is to be redeemed; it is a great and glorious work, and we are the instrumentalities by which it is to be done.

[2] The idea of black triangulation was first proposed by Professor George Shepperson in "Notes on Negro American Influences on the Emergence of African Nationalism," *Journal of African History,* I, 2 (1960), pp. 299–312. I have both modified and extended the idea here.
[3] Martin Delany, *The Condition, Elevation, Emigration, and Destiny of the Colored People of the United States* (New York: Arno Press and The New York Times, 1968), p. 183.

4

INTRODUCTION

This charge was soon to become a familiar one; it is to Delany's credit to have uttered it so early. But whatever the intrinsic and historic merit of Delany's work, it pales before the prodigious and eloquent efforts made by a truly Atlantic personality, Edward Wilmot Blyden. Blyden was active in a number of positions. Born in St. Thomas in the Danish West Indies in 1832, he went to the United States for an education, but discrimination in this country caused him to emigrate to Liberia in 1851. He variously was Liberian secretary of state, ambassador to the Court of Saint James, president of Liberia College, and minister of the interior.

Blyden figures most importantly in the development of an African black consciousness, in the creation of a spirit of black nationalism. Labeled "Pioneer West African Nationalist" and "The First African Personality," [4] Blyden dedicated his life to the political and ideological re-creation of an African world, one in which the black would find renewed dignity and purpose. Believing in the necessity of black repatriation, he envisioned a vast West African state, English-speaking but culturally African. As he initially witnessed the rapid emigration of blacks from the United States to Liberia in the years prior to the Civil War, he hopefully anticipated the demographic and territorial expansion of Liberia into that political form he desired to see shaped. When his hopes for this project were dashed, he encouraged British expansionism, seeing European imperialism as short-lived but potentially beneficial in creating an extended African political framework.

Blyden's ambitions for an African state were as premature as they were bold, but, through his prescience and perseverance, he prepared the way for Pan-Africanism, signaled the need to retain and respect basic African institutions, and provided some, indeed many of the basic tenets for the ideology of blackness—and in rather well-developed form.

Blyden believed the African would have to define himself with respect to his environment, his past, and in contrast with the European. Although he did not question the increasingly popular thought of the time that races were distinctively different and that racial purity was a desideratum if not a virtue, he rejected the notion that the white race was in the ascendant. Each race had its contribution to make, each had its own well-delineated cultural contours. For the

---

[4] The first term was employed in an article by Hollis Lynch, "Edward W. Blyden: Pioneer West African Nationalist," *Journal of African History*, VI, 3 (1965), pp. 373–388; the second term is part of a chapter title in Robert July's *The Origin of Modern African Thought* (New York: Frederick A. Praeger, Inc., 1967), Chapter 11.

African, the salient characteristics were spiritual and communal: a developed sense of religion and a harmonious appreciation of nature, a social system based on community and cooperation.

While Blyden was joined by other contemporary West Africans like the Gold Coast lawyer Casely Hayford and the Nigerian minister Mojola Agbebi in asserting the need to recast the attitudes of the time—European-derived practices and institutions withal—in the African idiom and life-style, Blyden still deserves the central position assigned him in the development of modern African thought: he had an exceptionally clear vision of the shape-to-be of modern Africa and of black dignity; and he structured this vision in meaningful and inspirational terms.

The one person at the end of this era who not only rivaled but also excelled Blyden in terms of intellectual prowess and output was W. E. B. Du Bois who, from the North American continent, personally became the gravitational center of much political organization and thought. Du Bois's life runs parallel with most of the exciting development of the black cultural and political movements; in some large measure his own biography is a history of this movement. His intellectual odyssey, so sensitively described in his autobiographical *Dusk at Dawn*, took him from comfortable origins in Great Barrington, Massachusetts, to Fisk University, Harvard, then the University of Berlin, and back to the United States and the South with an appointment at Atlanta University. He gained considerable notoriety and some fame in his intellectual opposition to Booker T. Washington. Du Bois firmly disagreed with Washington's segregationist philosophy, expressed best in his famous statement made in Atlanta in 1895: "In all things purely social we can be as separate as the five fingers, and yet one as the hand in all things essential to material progress." For Du Bois the solution for the black man was not subordinate segregation, but equal integration, guarantee of the basic constitutional rights of any American.

While Du Bois later adopted a more radical position, he remained constantly concerned with the actual condition and future direction of his people. His intellectual pursuits led him to range from the writing of one of the first scholarly interpretations of the slave trade to one of the first sociological studies of American minorities. But his most inspirational work was the volume of essays issued in 1903 under the title *The Souls of Black Folk*. In this work Du Bois presented his reader with a rich appreciation of the culture and the past of the black. He also expressed his hope in complementary pluralism: ". . . that some day on American soil two world-races may give each to each those characteristics both so sadly lack." And yet he also realized with remarkable vision that, tragically, "the problem of the twentieth century is the problem of the color-line."

Marcus Garvey recognized the implications of this line. Garvey is no doubt the most colorful and the most controversial of the figures who helped form the ideology of blackness. From humble beginnings in Jamaica, he rose to be head of the United Negro Improvement Association, which attained a membership of some six million blacks in 1923, and he also declared himself Provisional President of the Republic of Africa. Within another decade he was to slip from public notice, derisively discarded, a victim of public opinion, careless finances, and, perhaps, overwhelming *hubris*.

However, no one can doubt the peculiar greatness of Garvey, his ability to have sensed a new mood, to have encouraged it and provided it with attractive, if pretentious form. For Garvey was one of the New Negroes determined to replace subservience with assertiveness, to state that black is beautiful, and to demonstrate that the black was vastly capable.

When he arrived in New York in 1916, he had already behind him an intensely active career; he now desired to give it new dimensions. Settling in Harlem, he encouraged black boot-strapping activities; founded his own newspaper; established the Black Star Steamship Line, a navigational company hopefully to relay men, goods, and ideas between New York, the Caribbean, and the West Coast of Africa. He also created a magnificent paper empire, complete with noble orders and resounding titles, and served by Black Cross nurses, an African Motor Corps, and a Royal African Guard. Something of an empire-in-exile, this elaborate but still ill-defined structure was one that corresponded to Garvey's Back-to-Africa ideas. He firmly believed that the future of the American black lay in exodus; hence he has been called the Black Moses.

Garvey, like Blyden before him and in contradistinction to Du Bois, believed in racial separatism. Indeed, he was opposed to miscegenation, looked upon mulattos with something bordering on disdain—and, in fact, had contemptuous words for Du Bois's rather fair complexion. A full-blooded black himself, he advocated racial purity and denounced the "hybrids of the Negro race." Such thinking won him the support of the Ku Klux Klan and several wealthy negrophobes, not an insignificant factor in his final political demise.

Garvey, in a rudimentary but forceful manner, combined a form of

Pan-Africanism with Black Power. His ideas were neither profound nor original, and have been treated to harsh criticism.[5] But whatever the simplistic and rough definitions of his thought, Garvey remains a most significant figure. He was a man of his times; his actions were evocations. He tended to waken numbers of blacks to the realization that their present unfortunate state could give way to a pride-ringed future. Moreover, he aroused more than passing concern among high authorities in the West African colonies. As he considered settling groups of his followers in Liberia and as his ideas began to attract African attention, he and his movement were viewed as a threat to the prevailing European colonial administrations. Garvey thus had a truly international impact, no matter how ephemeral it may have been.

With the cresting of the Garvey movement in the 1920's, the first transoceanic triangulation of black ideology was completed. Ideas had circulated from St. Thomas to Liberia, from Jamaica to New York, and from New York to West Africa. Whether political activists or not, whether black separatists or not, the cultural carriers of these ideas were all desirous of arousing a black consciousness, of giving new meaning to the black experience. Because of their efforts, the black man began to affirm his African heritage and to rejoice in it. Moreover, through their writings, the black community was provided with new cultural dimensions, and thus was in theory distinctly set apart from the white community. In short, a new political and social mood of international scope was being formed.

But it was the second process of triangulation, the Caribbean-Harlem-Paris lines, that provided a new lyrical mood, enriching the ideology of blackness with both an infusion of new artistic appreciation and an attempt at definition of a black aesthetic.

To define the Harlem renaissance is not easy; its literary expressions and the themes around which it was structured were varied; the personalities who formed a brilliant coterie—men like Claude McKay, Countee Cullen, Langston Hughes, James Weldon Johnson, and Arna Bontemps—were of different backgrounds and interests. But it was a concentration of talent, dedicated to introspection and redefinition, full of confidence and jubilation, and, ultimately, it provided the ideology of blackness with new, popular dimensions.

The vital center of this cultural outburst, with 135th Street between Lenox and Seventh avenues as its major axis, was in itself an

---

[5] See, for instance, Janheinz Jahn, *Neo-African Literature: A History of Black Writing* (New York: Grove Press, 1968), p. 168.

exciting fact. The growing concentration of blacks in Harlem was the result of war-induced work opportunities in the North; of black purchase of real estate in the area through early black capitalism, in some part derivative from Washington's philosophy; and of the attraction of New York as the nation's intellectual magnet. There in Harlem was created a new cultural center and a new awareness on the part of blacks of the range of their artistic talents and of the possibility of a renaissance.

"Within this area," wrote Alain Locke, professor at Howard University and an influential figure in the Harlem renaissance,[6]

> race sympathy and unity have determined a further fusion of sentiment and experience. So what began in terms of segregation becomes more and more, as its elements mix and react, the laboratory of a great race-welding.... In Harlem, Negro life is seizing upon its first chances for group expression and self-determination. It is—or promises at least to be—a race capital.

Out of Harlem emerged the rhapsodic phase of the ideology of blackness, a celebration of the distinctive and historically determined qualities of the black ethos. Fusing thought and experiences coming from the West Indies, from the South, from the Northern ghetto, and from the African past, the new literature of the New Negro was exploring what Langston Hughes has called "the soul world." Most of this work was of poetic expression and is, perhaps, typified if not climaxed in Countee Cullen's famous poem of exotic mood, "Heritage."

In much of this new poetic effort one finds early literary appreciation of what Léopold Sédar Senghor has called an "existential ontology," a unique sense of being, a subtly attuned personal rapport with nature, the participation in and joyous communion with the surrounding environment, the rhythmic expression of life. Here in Harlem, and in the works of the men who defined its culture, was the beginning of a black aesthetic; here was the beginning of a black language of poetic praise and ethnic glorification; and here was a conscious, if still innocent return to an African past that informed a black present.

The poetry of Harlem anticipated negritude in spirit, language, and structure. The cultural environment of Harlem anticipated that of Paris, where negritude was defined, by some ten years.

---

[6] Alain Locke, "The New Negro," in Locke, ed., *The New Negro* (New York: Johnson Reprint Corp., 1968), pp. 6–7.

INTRODUCTION

Paris responded enthusiastically to a Harlemlike mood which seized the city in the 1930's. Intimations of its development were obvious before then, however. Josephine Baker had already captured music hall audiences by the end of the first postwar decade; the black deputy from Senegal, Blaise Diagne, had become a familiar parliamentary figure; and the beguine, imported from Martinique, was being rhythmically beaten out in the cabarets and cafés with the same popular success that had accompanied the Charleston somewhat earlier. Of equal significance, the French public had become acquainted with the rich and varied historical background of black Africa through the efforts of the scholar-administrator Maurice Delafosse and through the publication, in 1921, of the impressive anthology of African folk literature amassed by the French author Blaise Cendrars.

Nevertheless, the date of the French African renaissance is best situated in the year 1931. In that year, all of these earlier conditioning factors were conjoined in the pretentious and important International Colonial Exposition which had proceeded from the mind of the great French colonial administrator, Marshal Hubert Lyautey, to sprawl across nearly three thousand acres of the Bois de Vincennes and so to bring the colonies to Paris. Amid an array of buildings garishly interpreted in the indigenous idiom, artists, dancers, and craftsmen from the various French overseas possessions performed for the Parisian crowds. "Has the Colonial Exposition taught the Parisians something new about the Negroes?" asked one editorial writer.

Whatever the answer to the question, the decade of the 1930's saw the ideology of blackness center in France and raise itself to the level of rapturous endorsement. A literary theme and style of blackness, negritude, was formulated, if essentially as a subject of poetic expression, also as a subject rich in philosophical implications. Its chief expositor, but not its originator, is Léopold Sédar Senghor: today poet-philosopher President of the Republic of Senegal, then a student in Paris experiencing the intellectual stimulation of that city and enduring the loneliness and social isolation that derived from his skin color.

If Senghor emerges as the giant figure, he was not alone. Surrounded by fellow colonial students, notably from the Caribbean possessions of France, he was part of a new generation away from home and increasingly conscious of the cultural ambivalence surrounding their situation as Africans in a country professing universalism of thought. As they reflected on their intellectual position, they turned inward and spiritually to a historical past and communal existence they felt had been denied them.

As vehicles for expression of these new sentiments, a number of literary magazines appeared. The longest in duration was *Le monde noir*, which progressed for six months with its announced objective "to give the intelligentsia of the black race and their partisans an official organ in which to publish their artistic, literary, and scientific works." Of greater significance was the most transitory, *Étudiant noir*, which emerged from the collaboration of Senghor, Léon Damas, and Aimé Césaire, the tripod of minds upon which negritude originally rested. It was the program of the publication "to rehabilitate the name, personality, and value of the Negro."

This Parisian-centered cultural endeavor, in its several forms, was doubly infused: first, with a new national consciousness emerging out of the French-speaking Caribbean islands, and from Haiti in particular; and second, with the literature and ideas from Harlem.

Of the points in the second cultural triangulation, the one least marked is that of the Haitian renaissance, a most interesting and lamentably ignored occurrence. It began with the occupation of the island country by American Marines in 1915, an action which, because of its arrogance, aroused both frustration and anger among Haitian intellectuals. As one of them, Jean Price-Mars, has commented: unable to combat the Marines militarily, the Haitians fought back culturally.[7] A number of literary and historical societies were formed, as were literary journals, the most significant of which was *Les griots*. It proclaimed: "We other, we Haitian griots,[8] must sing the splendor of our countryside, the sweetness of our April sunsets, ... the beauty of our women, the exploits of our ancestors." As the quotation would indicate, and as Price-Mars asserts, the new effort was a rejection of Western culture and an expression of what has been variously called indigenism, Haitianism, Africanism. No person was more responsible for the Haitian appreciation of the last "ism" than Price-Mars who, as ethnographer, diplomat, and nationalist, urged his people to investigate their African past and to honor it.

Yet this awareness of and interest in a new Caribbean cultural

---

[7] Jean Price-Mars, *De Saint-Dominique à Haiti; essai sur la culture, les arts, et la littérature* (Paris: Présence Africaine, 1959), pp. 44–45.
[8] The term "griot" refers to that person in West Africa who performed a troubadourlike function in singing of the glories of the past and the heroic deeds of his ancestors.

INTRODUCTION

experience, while viewed with enthusiasm by most of the belletristic colonial students living in Paris at the time, was neither so influential nor so formative of negritude as was the work exported directly from Harlem and translated into the hearts and minds of young blacks in Paris. Senghor himself has acknowledged that, between 1929 and 1934, he had come into contact with the writings of Claude McKay, Jean Toomer, Langston Hughes, and Countee Cullen in a literary salon where American, Caribbean, and African blacks met.[9] The sense of rhythm, the return to the African past, the imagery—these were qualities exhibited by this poetry which Senghor appreciated and emulated—although it would be most unjust to suggest that his own poetic works were seriously derivative.

As a literary movement, negritude was founded by three aforementioned poets: Léon Damas from French Guiana, Aimé Césaire from Martinique (who, incidentally, first employed the term), and Léopold Senghor from Senegal. The first contributed a new sense of poetic rhythm, particularly a Caribbean dancelike quality to his work; the second worked the French language to new evocative heights, revealing an exotic and passion-burnished world that was imaginatively far removed from the European; the third brought his poetry back to Africa, where it captured the movement of the dancer and the beat of the tom-tom.[10]

But negritude was not simply a stylistic matter. First employed on the eve of the Second World War, the word came to embrace a variety of meanings after the war, particularly as a cultural weapon with which to combat or complement Westernization and as a source of inspiration with which to greet a newly emerging African world. Now variously connoting skin-color, outlook, feelings, mores, even historical traditions, negritude came near to being a cultural cosmology. In Senghor's own definition, "Negritude is the cultural patrimony, the values, and, above all, the spirit of Negro-African civilization." Social-psychologically, it was the African's affective appreciation of nature; it was expressive of an existential ontology, understanding, and enjoyment of a world that was known more through the reason of the heart and soul than through the calculated reason of the intelligence. Politically, it came to be equated with

---

[9] See his statement in Lilyan Kesteloot, Les écrivains noirs de langue française (Brussels: Université libre de Bruxelles, 1963), p. 63. Also see Senghor's assessment of the literary influence of the Harlem renaissance poets in his "Trois poètes négro-américains," Poésie, 45, No. 23 (February–March 1945), pp. 32–33.
[10] On this subject see Kesteloot, op. cit., p. 124, and Jahn, op. cit., p. 244.

a particular form of African socialism, communally structured and marked by its lack of Marxist-analyzed class conflict; but more immediately, it was seen, at least by Jean-Paul Sartre, as an "antiracist racism," a necessary response of black affirmation to white denial, a means to social rehabilitation in which all that was denigrated by the European was now dignified by the African. To Senghor, it was Africa's hallmark, indelibly stamped, authentically registered; it was Africa's contribution to all of humanity, a gift by which to enlarge and enrich the entire universe of mind and heart.

Coincidental with the period of decolonization, negritude was impressed upon African thought, and thus provided a cultural base for much of early subsaharan African nationalism. Moreover, it appealingly made its way to the United States—again an obvious suggestion of the brisk transatlantic commerce in ideas. A few black American writers have found it valuable as a literary guide and a source of literary inspiration; a few others have considered it the basis for American black culture as well as for African.

Negritude has thus assumed the most universal proportions and the widest degree of acceptance of any aspect of the ideology of blackness. Its perigee was reached in 1956 when the first International Congress of Negro Writers and Artists met in Paris. With such illustrious participants as Senghor, Richard Wright, Price-Mars, and Césaire, the meeting was high tribute to the now profound interest in black culture and to its tricontinental pervasiveness. The final resolution of the Congress recognized this new mood when it asserted "... the imperious necessity of proceeding toward a rediscovery of historical truth and a reevaluation of Negro cultures."

Perhaps this Congress was, metaphorically, the third and terminal point around which the second black triangulation occurred. For with African political independence and the newly pressing problems of economic modernization, negritude on the African continent and even in Europe declined in significance and in the amount of effective intellectual attention it received.

Once again, the scene of cultural activity is the United States. With the success of the African independence movements, with the climaxing of the Civil Rights movement, and with the rather impressive degree of popularity which now greeted the Nation of Islam movement founded by Elijah Muhammed in the 1930's, a new black consciousness and political activism developed here. Particularly since the term "Black Power" started to gain in popular appeal, largely through the efforts of Stokely Carmichael, radical blacks in this country have set about to define and create a particular, supportive culture. As Floyd McKissick, former National Director of the Congress of Racial Equality, has succinctly stated:[11]

> The Black Power movement seeks to instill in the hearts of black people everywhere, a deep pride and awareness of the beauty of being black. Black consciousness must become a way of life.

An even more radical interpretation of the function of black awareness suggests that the success of political nationalism is dependent upon a mass that has been culturally galvanized. As Ron Karenga, one of the most articulate and controversial of contemporary black nationalists, has asserted:[12]

> We have always said, and continue to say, that the battle we are now waging is the battle for the minds of Black people, and that if we lose this battle, we cannot win the violent one.

It must be obvious that, however interpreted, the ideology of blackness is a major factor in plans for black political liberation in the United States.

What makes the American ideological situation so perplexing and frequently fragmented is, of course, the unique historical and spatial relationships of the blacks to the rest of the community. First, there is the ideological necessity to determine the degree to which black society may derive from or depend upon a larger American society. James Baldwin argues that "the Negro has been formed by this nation, for better or for worse, and does not belong to any other."[13] Does such an assertion therefore imply that Africa, which has been the lodestar for so much of the black ideological effort, can only provide historical inspiration at best to any black American cultural endeavor? Malcolm X, the most forceful and inspirational of black radicals, denied such an implication. He stated that "physically we Afro-Americans might remain in America, fighting for our Constitutional rights, but that philosophically and culturally we Afro-Americans badly needed to 'return'

---

[11] Floyd McKissick, "Why We Still Haven't Overcome," *Rights and Reviews*, Vol. 3 (Winter 1966–67), p. 7.
[12] Ron Karenga, "Ron Karenga and Black Cultural Nationalism," *Negro Digest* (January 1968), p. 5.
[13] James Baldwin, *The Fire Next Time* (New York: Delta, 1964), p. 95.

to Africa—and to develop a working unity in the framework of Pan-Africanism." [14]

Second, there is the problem of meaning which surrounds the idea of "colonial situation." As a general term it is image-inspiring, bringing into view patterns of political domination and racial oppression. But the territorial expropriation and exploitation which the term also connotes in the African context are missing from the American one. While some enthusiasm residually remains attached to the Back-to-Africa movement, there is no clearly defined land to which blacks might collectively repair, if they so desired. Elijah Muhammed has urged his followers, "Let's unite into a great nation"; but the locus of his aspiration remains ill-defined and is much more spiritual than spatial. While the National Black Government Conference, meeting in Detroit in 1968, formed in theory a "Republic of New Africa," to be carved out of the South, the term "nation" still has more a rhetorical than a territorial meaning at present.

Third, there is the consideration of the particularism of black cultural nationalism as new political dimensions of radicalism are being defined. The Black Panthers, for instance, now accept a solidarity of interest and are tending to make a common cause with representatives of other groups in this country and abroad who feel oppressed; thus, in political commitment, they are going far beyond the "brother on the block," to employ Bobby Seale's phrase.

Yet, regardless of such obvious problems and concerns, the importance of black culture and black nationalism on the contemporary American scene cannot be denied. Black studies programs, Afro hairdos, and dashikis are but the most obvious manifestations of a new interest in and a new attempt to define the ideology of blackness. Its more radical advocates hope that, through a well-defined black culture, a true black community will emerge and will acquire definite purpose, perhaps as a distinct ethnic group within American society, or perhaps as a nation without it.

In the last two decades, as it has risen in popularity and forcefulness of expression, the ideology of blackness has met criticism within the black community on both sides of the Atlantic. Negritude, both as literary and philosophical doctrine, has incurred the most severe criticism. Essentially characteristic of intellectuals coming from former French West Africa, it has been denounced by many English-speaking Africans as romantic and antiquarian, not socially conscious and politically relevant. By seeking to understand the

[14] *The Autobiography of Malcolm X* (New York: Grove Press, 1966), p. 350.

African soul, and by examining a precolonial past, it has had a distractive effect and also has tended to freeze Africa in time; so runs one argument. Neither revolutionary nor modernizing in purpose and effect, negritude sings praise of a pastoral way of life and thus deflects political attention from the crucial issues of the day; so runs a concomitant argument. Finally, there are those who believe that negritude has simply invested old European prejudices about the African with new value: the African is still defined as the child of nature.

If political activists like the Martiniquan Frantz Fanon and the Dahomean Stanislas Adotevi are bothered by negritude because it is more directed to a universalized African past than to a radicalized African future, and because it is more concerned with oceanic feelings about blackness than about political and social realities, some literary critics, like the South African Ezekiel Mphahalele, are concerned with the romanticism in which negritude is cloaked. Arguing against any attempt to establish negritude as a principle of art, they assert the need for the artist not to engage in poetic idealization but rather to seek all themes and styles that will explain best the human condition as he knows it. Thus, for such critics, negritude may have been a valuable political pose in the period of decolonization but serves poorly as a contemporary political or literary doctrine.

Yet even the intense debate which whirled around negritude has now abated in Africa. The first Pan-African Cultural Conference, held in Algiers in the summer of 1969, witnessed forceful cultural condemnations of negritude. Today, those African critics who look favorably on negritude frequently see it as a historically dated phenomenon. It reflected an intellectual reorientation for many French-educated Africans who were, in effect, returning to their native land.

On this side of the Atlantic, criticism of the ideology of blackness has not been totally dissimilar in form or degree to that visited on negritude. While many literary critics support the idea, others seriously question it. When asked if he saw any future for the establishment of black aesthetics, the well-known critic and author Saunders Redding replied: "No. Not in America. Besides aesthetics has no racial, national, or geographical boundaries. Beauty and truth, the principal components of aesthetics, are universal."[15] And while

---

[15] Statement quoted in "A Survey of Black Writers' Views on Literary Lions and Values," *Negro Digest* (January 1969), p. 12.

the Black Panthers have spoken of and supported black nationalism, Bobby Seale, in his recently published *Seize the Time* has clearly indicated his disfavor with avid black cultural nationalists such as Ron Karenga.

Whatever its historical significance, the ideology of blackness as a tricontinental cultural phenomenon has demonstrated the common contours of the problems affecting the descendants of the uprooted Africans. Yet as an ideology it certainly does not rival the major ideologies, like Marxism, for instance, in doctrinal coherency or universality of impact. If anything, it is more akin to the romantic phase of European nationalism, with its salient characteristics being of a literary and cultural nature rather than of a political-institutional sort. Like the Germanic response to Napoleonic France, blackness is a reaction against what is considered cultural imperialism derived from the ethnocentric assumption of the universality of principles and institutions defined by and viable for one single people.

The search for the spiritual force needed to inspire the realization of an organic community may run counter to the liberal theories of political and social assimilation in this country and to certain colonial theories represented by slogans like "white man's burden" and "civilizing mission." But in a growingly pluralistic world, disenchanted with the dominance of Western materialism, such a search does not seem inappropriate. It may, however, be doomed to political futility. In Africa, the only extensive organizing cultural principle in recent history was anti-imperialism; this has now been replaced by the fracturing process which nation-building engenders. In the United States, egalitarian desires still predominate among the major portion of the black population, while disunity of black radical and nationalist movements still disallows for an organized cultural front.

The ultimate impact of the ideology of blackness will probably not be contingent upon political success, however. The thought that it has provoked has had a meaningful, popular impact, if not the enthusiastic support of impressively large numbers. To date, it has chiefly been an expression of an intellectual elite attempting to redefine the world in which they live and would like to live. As an ethical, literary, and ethnically inspirational force, the ideology of blackness has none the less already contributed importantly to the growing pluralism and cultural reevaluation occurring in our times.

PART I

THE FORMATIVE PERIOD
Toward Cultural Definition

MARTIN ROBINSON DELANY

Now considered by many to be the first American black nationalist, Delany had a varied and interesting career. Born in 1812, in what has become West Virginia, he began his active career in Pittsburgh in 1843, when he founded one of the first black publications, *Mystery*. He met Frederick Douglass, who was interested in Delany's work and who made him the editor of Douglass' *The North Star*, a position Delany held for a period of nearly a year. In 1859 he headed an exploratory expedition up the Niger and returned to the United States by way of England and Canada. During the Civil War he served as a major on the Northern side, and after the war he worked in the South Carolina Freedmen's Bureau. He even ran for political office as a candidate for lieutenant governor in South Carolina under the banner of the short-lived Independent Radical Party in 1874. In 1879 he published his *Principia of Ethnology: The Origin of Races and Color*. He died in 1885.

Delany's major work, *The Condition, Elevation, Emigration, and Destiny of the Colored People of the United States*, which was first published in 1852, treated three subjects: first, the condition of the black in the United States; second, the aptitudes and achievements of the blacks in various professions; and, third, emigrationist solutions to the problems with which the black was confronted. It is the third portion of the book, in which Delany suggests the possibility of mass emigration to some spot in Latin America, that has garnered considerable attention; but perhaps even more has been concentrated on the brief appendix, which suggests the possibility of the establishment of an American black republic in East Africa. Delany's turn to emigration, to a sort of early Back-to-Africa move, resulted more from disappointment than ardent desire: the realization of the intensive and enduring racism in the United States.

FURTHER READING: Theodore Draper. "The Father of Black Nationalism," *The New York Review of Books*, March 12, 1970, pp. 33–41.

Martin Robinson Delany

From The Condition, Elevation, Emigration, and Destiny of the Colored People of the United States

The utility of men in their private capacity as citizens is of no less import than that of any other department of the community in which they live; indeed, the fitness of men for positions in the body politic, can only be justly measured by their qualification as citizens. And we may safely venture the declaration, that in the history of the world, there has never been a nation, that among the oppressed class of inhabitants—a class entirely ineligible to any political position of honor, profit, or trust—wholly discarded from the recognition of citizens' rights—not even permitted to carry the mail, nor drive a mail coach—there never has, in the history of nations, been any people thus situated, who has made equal progress in attainments with the colored people of the United States. It would be as unnecessary as it is impossible, to particularize all the individuals; we shall therefore be satisfied with a classification and a few individual cases. Our history in this country is well known, and quite sufficiently treated on in these pages already, without the necessity of repetition here; it is enough to know that by the most cruel acts of injustice and crime, our forefathers were forced by small numbers, and enslaved in the country—the great body now to the number of three millions and a half, still groaning in bondage—that the half million now free, are the descendants of the few who by various means, are fortunate enough to gain their liberty from Southern bondage—that no act of general emancipation has ever taken place, and no chance as yet for a general rebellion—we say in view of all these facts, we proceed to give a cursory history of the attainments—the civil, social, business and

---

Source: Martin Robinson Delany, The Condition, Elevation, Emigration, and Destiny of the Colored People of the United States, Arno Press Edition, 1968, pp. 85–87, 209–210. Reprinted by permission of the publisher.

professional, and literary attainments of colored men and women, and challenge comparison with the world—according to circumstances—in times past and present.

Though shorn of their strength, disarmed of manhood, and stripped of every right, encouraged by the part performed by their brethren and fathers in the Revolutionary struggle—with no records of their deeds in history, and no means of knowing them save orally, as overheard from the mouths of their oppressors, and tradition as kept up among themselves—that memorable event, had not yet ceased its thrill through the new-born nation, until a glimmer of hope—a ray of light had beamed forth, and enlightened minds thought to be in total darkness. Minds of no ordinary character, but those which embraced business, professions, and literature—minds, which at once grasped the earth, encompassed the seas, soared into the air, and mounted the skies. And it is nonetheless creditable to the colored people, that among those who have stood the most conspicuous and shone the brightest in the earliest period of our history, there are those of pure and unmixed African blood. A credit—but that which is creditable to the African, cannot disgrace any into whose veins his blood may chance to flow. The elevation of the colored man can only be completed by the elevation of the pure descendants of Africa; because to deny his equality, is to deny in a like proportion, the equality of all those mixed with the African organization; and to establish his inferiority will be to degrade every person related to him by consanguinity; therefore, to establish the equality of the African with the European race, establishes the equality of every person intermediate between the two races. This establishes beyond contradiction, the general equality of men.

* * *

Every people should be the originators of their own designs, the projectors of their own schemes, and creators of the events that lead to their destiny—the consummation of their desires.

Situated as we are, in the United States, many, and almost insurmountable obstacles present themselves. We are four-and-a-half millions in numbers, free and bond; six hundred thousand free, and three-and-a-half millions bond.

We have native hearts and virtues, just as other nations; which in their pristine purity are noble, potent, and worthy of example. We are a nation within a nation—as the Poles in Russia, the Hungarians in Austria, the Welsh, Irish, and Scotch in the British dominions.

But we have been, by our oppressors, despoiled of our purity, and corrupted in our native characteristics, so that we have inherited their vices, and but few of their virtues, leaving us in character, really a *broken people*.

Being distinguished by complexion, we are still singled out—although having merged in the habits and customs of our oppressors—as a distinct nation of people; as the Poles, Hungarians, Irish, and others, who still retain their native peculiarities, of language, habits, and various other traits. The claims of no people, according to established policy and usage, are respected by any nation, until they are presented in a national capacity.

EDWARD WILMOT BLYDEN

When Blyden left his native St. Thomas in 1851 to seek an education in the United States, he had not anticipated being greeted with such intensive racist sentiment. As a result, he willingly left for Liberia when the American Colonization Society made his travel possible. In Liberia, he pursued an active and multifunctional career, beginning with his ordination as a Presbyterian minister. In 1861 he was made professor of Greek and Latin at Liberia College; three years later he became Liberian secretary of state and then ambassador to England in 1877. His active political career ended with his position as Liberian minister of the interior between 1881 and 1882. From 1871 on Blyden spent considerable time in Sierra Leone; he died in Freetown in 1912.

Blyden was an indefatigable author; he founded a short-lived newspaper called *The Negro* and helped found *The West African Reporter* and the *Sierra Leone Weekly News*. His contributions to *Fraser's Magazine*, a distinguished British quarterly, won him wide attention and acclaim.

Blyden, upholding the notion of racial separatism, believed in American black emigration to Africa. He appraised the far-reaching African past and, examining Egyptian history in this light, appreciated Islam and compared it very favorably to Christianity.

His *Christianity, Islam, and the Negro Race*, published in 1887, consists for the most part of articles reprinted from *Fraser's Magazine* and speeches made in Africa and the United States. Blyden's views and opinions in this volume ranged far and wide, but he was consistent in upholding the need for racial solidarity and in emphasizing the values of African customs and institutions. Although he wrote other volumes, *Christianity, Islam, and the Negro Race* remains his most important, indeed one of the most important, contributions to the ideology of blackness.

FURTHER READING: Hollis R. Lynch. *Edward W. Blyden, Pan-Negro Patriot, 1832–1912.* New York: Oxford University Press, 1967.

Edward Wilmot Blyden

From *Christianity, Islam, and the Negro Race*

Address delivered January 5, 1881, "The Aims and Methods of a Liberal Education for Africans."

To a certain extent—perhaps to a very important extent—Negroes trained on the soil of Africa have the advantage of those trained in foreign countries; but in all, as a rule, the intellectual and moral results, thus far, have been far from satisfactory. There are many men of book learning, but few, very few, of any *capability*—even few who have that amount, or that sort, of culture, which produces self-respect, confidence in one's self, and efficiency in work. Now, why is this? The evil, it is considered, lies in the system and methods of European training to which Negroes are, everywhere in Christian lands, subjected, and which everywhere affects them unfavorably. Of a different race, different susceptibility, different bent of character from that of the European, they have been trained under influences in many respects adapted only to the Caucasian race. Nearly all the books they read, the very instruments of their culture, have been such as to force them from the groove which is natural to them, where they would be strong and effective, without furnishing them with any avenue through which they may move naturally and free from obstruction. Christian and so-called civilized Negroes live, for the most part, in foreign countries, where they are only passive spectators of the deeds of a foreign race; and where, with other impressions which they receive from without, an element of doubt as to their own capacity and their own destiny is fastened upon them, and inheres in their intellectual and social constitution. They deprecate their own individuality, and would escape from it if they could. And in countries like this, where they are free from the hampering surroundings of an

---

Source: Edward Wilmot Blyden, *Christianity, Islam, and the Negro Race* (Edinburgh: University of Edinburgh Press, 1967), pp. 75–79, 91–93, 124–129, 350–354.

alien race, they still read and study the books of foreigners, and form their idea of everything that man may do, or ought to do, according to the standard held up in those teachings. Hence, without the physical or mental aptitude for the enterprises which they are taught to admire and revere, they attempt to copy and imitate them, and share the fate of all copyists and imitators. Bound to move on a lower level, they acquire and retain a practical inferiority, transcribing, very often, the faults rather than the virtues of their models.

Besides this result of involuntary impressions, they often receive direct teachings which are not only incompatible with, but destructive of, their self-respect.

In all English-speaking countries the mind of the intelligent Negro child revolts against the descriptions given in elementary books—geographies, travels, histories—of the Negro; but, though he experiences an instinctive revulsion from these caricatures and misrepresentations, he is obliged to continue, as he grows in years, to study such pernicious teachings. After leaving school he finds the same things in newspapers, in reviews, in novels, in *quasi* scientific works; and after a while—*saepe cadendo*—they begin to seem to him the proper things to say and to feel about his race, and he accepts what, at first, his fresh and unbiased feelings naturally and indignantly repelled. Such is the effect of repetition.

Having embraced, or at least assented, to these errors and falsehoods about himself, he concludes that his only hope of rising in the scale of respectable manhood is to strive after whatever is most unlike himself and most alien to his peculiar tastes. And whatever his literary attainments or acquired ability, he fancies that he must grind at the mill which is provided for him, putting in the material furnished to his hands, bringing no contribution from his own field; and of course nothing comes out but what is put in. Thus he can never bring any real assistance to the European. He can never attain to that essence of progress which Mr. Herbert Spencer describes as *difference;* and therefore, he never acquires the self-respect or self-reliance of an independent contributor. He is not an independent help, only a subordinate help; so that the European feels that he owes him no debt, and moves on in contemptuous indifference of the Negro, teaching him to contemn himself.

Those who have lived in civilized communities, where there are different races, know the disparaging views which are entertained of the blacks by their neighbours—and often, alas! by themselves. The standard of all physical and intellectual excellencies in the present civilization being the white complexion, whatever deviates from that favoured colour is proportionally depreciated, until the black, which is opposite, becomes not only the most unpopular but the most unprofitable colour. Black men, and especially black women, in such communities, experience the greatest imaginable inconvenience. They never feel at home. In the depth of their being they always feel themselves strangers in the land of their exile, and the only escape from this feeling is to escape from themselves. And this feeling of self-depreciation is not diminished as I have intimated above, by the books they read. Women, especially, are fond of reading novels and light literature; and it is in these writings that flippant and eulogistic reference is constantly made to the superior physical and mental characteristics of the Caucasian race, which, by contrast, suggest the inferiority of other races—especially of that race which is furthest removed from it in appearance.

It is painful in America to see the efforts which are made by Negroes to secure outward conformity to the appearance of the dominant race.

This is by no means surprising; but what is surprising is that, under the circumstances, any Negro has retained a particle of self-respect. Now in Africa, where the colour of the majority is black, the fashion in personal matters is naturally suggested by the personal characteristics of the race, and we are free from the necessity of submitting to the use of "incongruous feathers awkwardly stuck on." Still, we are held in bondage by our indiscriminate and injudicious use of a foreign literature; and we strive to advance by the methods of a foreign race. In this effort we struggle with the odds against us. We fight at the disadvantage which David would have experienced in Saul's armour. The African must advance by methods of his own. He must possess a power distinct from that of the European. It has been proved that he knows how to take advantage of European culture, and that he can be benefited by it. This proof was perhaps necessary, but it is not sufficient. We must show that we are able to go alone, to carve out our own way. We must not be satisfied that, in this nation, European influence shapes our polity, makes our laws, rules in our tribunals, and impregnates our social atmosphere. We must not suppose that the Anglo-Saxon methods are final, that there is nothing for us to find for our own guidance, and that we have nothing to teach the world. There is inspiration for us also. We must study our brethren in the interior, who know better than we do the laws of growth for the race. We see among them the rudiments of that which, with fair play and opportunity, will develop into important and effective agencies for our work. We look too much to foreigners, and are dazzled almost to blindness by their exploits—so as to fancy that they have exhausted the possibilities of humanity. In our estimation they, like Longfellow's Iagoo, have done and can do everything better than anybody else:

> Never heard he an adventure
> But himself had made a greater;
> Never any deed of daring,
> But himself had done a bolder
> Never any marvellous story
> But himself could tell a stranger.
> No one ever shot an arrow
> Half so far and high as he had;
> Ever caught so many fishes,
> Ever killed so many reindeer,
> Ever trapped so many beaver.
> None could run so fast as he could;
> None could dive so deep as he could;
> None could swim so far as he could;
> None had made so many journeys;
> None had seen so many wonders,
> As this wonderful Iagoo.

But there are possibilities before us not yet dreamed of by the Iagoos of civilisation. Dr. Alexander Winchell, professor in one of the American universities—who has lately written a book, in the name of Science, in which he reproduces all the old slanders against the Negro, and writes of the African at home as if Livingstone, Barth, Stanley, and Cameron had never written—mentions it, as one of the evidences of Negro inferiority, that in "Liberia he is indifferent to the benefits of civilization." I stand here to-day to justify and commend the Negro of Liberia—and of everywhere else in Africa—for rejecting with scorn, "always and every time," the "benefits" of civilization whose theories are to degrade him in the scale of humanity, and of which such sciolists as Dr. Winchell are the exponents and representative elements. We recommend all Africans to treat such "benefits" with even more decided "indifference" than that with which the guide in Dante treated the despicable herd—

> Non ragionam di lor, ma guarda, e passa.

Those of us who have travelled in foreign countries, and who witness the general results of European influence along this coast, have many reasons for misgivings and reserves and anxieties about European civilization for this country. Things which have been of great advantage to Europe may work ruin to us; and there is often such a striking resemblance, or such a close connection between the hurtful and the beneficial, that we are not always able to discriminate. I have heard of a native in one of the settlements on the coast who, having grown up in the use of the simple but efficient remedies of the country doctors, and having prospered in business, conceived the idea that he must avail himself of the medicines he saw used by the European traders. Suffering from sleeplessness he was advised to take Dover's powders, but, in his inexperience, took instead an overdose of morphine, and next morning he was a corpse. So we have reason to apprehend that in our indiscriminate appropriations of European agencies or methods in our political, educational, and social life, we are often imbibing overdoses of morphine, when we fancy we are only taking Dover's powders!

And it is for this reason, while we are anxious for immigration from America and desirous that the immigrants shall push as fast as possible into the interior, that we look with anxiety and concern at the difficulties and troubles which must arise from their misconception of the work to be done in this country. I apprehend that in their progress towards the interior there will be friction, irritations, and conflicts; and our brethren, in certain portions of the United States, are, at this moment, witnessing a state of things among their superiors which they will naturally want to reproduce in this country, and which, if reproduced here, will utterly extinguish the flickering light of the Line Star, and close forever this open door of Christian civilization into Africa.

Mr. Matthew Arnold reminds us that when someone talked to Themistocles of an art of memory, he answered, "Teach me rather to forget." The full meaning of this aspiration must be realized in the life of the Christian Negro before he can become a full man, or a successful worker in his fatherland.

*   *   *

As those who have suffered affliction in a foreign land, we have no antecedents from which to gather inspiration.

All our traditions and experiences are connected with a foreign race. We have no poetry or philosophy but that of our taskmasters. The songs that live in our ears and are often on our lips are the songs which we heard sung by those who shouted while we groaned and lamented. They sang of their history, which was the history of our degradation. They recited their triumphs, which contained the records of our humiliation. To our great misfortune, we learned their prejudices and their passions, and thought we had their aspirations and their power. Now, if we are to make an independent nation—a strong nation—we must listen to the songs of our unsophisticated brethren as they sing of their history, as they tell of their traditions, of the wonderful and mysterious events of their tribal or national life, of the achievements of what we call their superstitions; we must lend a ready ear to the ditties of the Kroomen who pull our boats, of the Pessah and Golah men, who till our farms; we must read the compositions, rude as we may think them, of the Mandingoes and the Veys. We shall in this way get back the strength of the race, like the giant of the ancients, who always gained strength, for his conflict with Hercules, whenever he touched his Mother Earth.

And this is why we want the College away from the seaboard —with its constant intercourse with foreign manners and low foreign ideas—that we may have free and uninterrupted intercourse with the intelligent among the tribes of the interior; that the students, even from the books to which they will be allowed access, may conveniently flee to the forests and fields of Manding and the Niger, and mingle with our brethren and gather fresh inspiration and fresh and living ideas.

It is the complaint of the intelligent Negro in America that the white people pay no attention to his suggestions or his writings; but this is only because he has nothing new to say—nothing that they have not said before him, and that they cannot say better than he can. Let us depend upon it, that the emotions and thoughts which are natural to us command the curiosity and respect of others far more than the showy display of any mere acquisitions which we have derived from them, and which they know depend more upon our memory than upon any real capacity. What we must follow is all that concerns our individual growth. Let us do our own work and we shall be strong and worthy of respect; try to do the work of others, and we shall be weak and contemptible. There is magnetism in original action, in self-trust, which others cannot resist. I think we mistake the meaning of the lines of the poet [Longfellow] which are so often quoted—

> Lives of great men all remind us
> We can make our lives sublime,
> And, departing, leave behind us
> Footprints on the sands of time.

How shall we make our "lives sublime"? Not by imitating others, but by doing well our own part as they did theirs. We are to study the "footprints" that when we are "forlorn," or have been "shipwrecked," we may "take heart again"; not to put our own feet in the impressions previously made, for by so doing we should be compelled at times to lengthen, and at times to shorten our pace—sometimes to make the strides of Hiawatha, and sometimes to crawl—and thus not only cut a most ungainly figure, but accomplish nothing, either for ourselves or the world.

"Whilst I read the poets," says Emerson—

> I think that nothing new can be said about morning and evening; but when I see the day break, I am not reminded of these Homeric or Shakespearian or Miltonic or Chaucerian pictures. No; but I am cheered by the moist, warm, glittering, budding, melodius hour, that takes down the narrow walls of my soul, and extends its life and pulsation to the very horizon. *That* is morning—to cease for a bright hour to be a prisoner of the sickly body, and to become as large as Nature.

We have a great work before us, a work unique in the history of the world, which others who appreciate its vastness and importance, envy us the privilege of doing. The world is looking at this Republic to see whether "order and law, religion and morality, the rights of conscience, the rights of persons, and the rights of property," may all be secured and preserved by a government administered entirely by Negroes.

Let us show ourselves equal to the task.

The time is past when we can be content with putting forth elaborate arguments to prove our equality with foreign races. Those who doubt our capacity are more likely to be convinced of their error by the exhibition, on our part, of those qualities of energy and enterprise which will enable us to occupy the extensive field before us for our own advantage and the advantage of humanity—for the purposes of civilization, of science, of good government, and of progress generally —than by any mere abstract argument about the equality of races. The suspicions disparaging to us will be dissipated only by the exhibition of the indisputable realities of a lofty manhood as they may be illustrated in successful efforts to build up a nation, to wrest from Nature her secrets, to lead the van of progress in this country, and to regenerate a continent.

EDWARD WILMOT BLYDEN

From a discourse delivered before the American Colonization Society, May 1880, "Ethiopia Stretching Out Her Hands Unto God; or, Africa's Service to the World."

The exiled Negro, then, has a home in Africa. Africa is his, if he will. He may ignore it. He may consider that he is divested of any right to it; but this will not alter his relations to that country, or impair the integrity of his title. He may be content to fight against the fearful odds in this country; but he is the proprietor of a vast domain. He is entitled to a whole continent by his constitution and antecedents. Those who refuse, at the present moment, to avail themselves of their inheritance think they do so because they believe that they are progressing in this country. There has, no doubt, been progress in many respects in their condition here. I would not, for one moment, say anything that would cast a shadow upon their hopes, or blight, in the slightest degree, their anticipations. I could wish that they might realize to the fullest extent their loftiest aspirations. It is indeed impossible not to sympathize with the intelligent Negro, whose imagination, kindled by the prospects and possibilities of this great country, the land of his birth, makes him desire to remain and share in its future struggles and future glories. But he still suffers from many drawbacks. The stranger visiting this land and going among its coloured inhabitants, and reading their newspapers, still hears the wail of slavery. The wail of physical suffering has been exchanged for the groans of an intellectual, social, and ecclesiastical ostracism. Not long since the touching appeal of a coloured man, almost in *forma pauperis*, before a great ecclesiastical assembly for equal rights in the Church, was wafted over the country, and sent its thrilling tones into many a heart, but yet the only response has been the reverberation of the echo. And who cannot understand the meaning of the hesitancy on the part of the powers that be to grant the appeal? "He who runs may read."

As a result of their freedom and enlarged education, the descendants of Africa in this country are beginning to feel themselves straitened. They are beginning to feel that only in Africa will they find the sphere of their true activity. And it is a significant fact that this impulse is coming from the Southern states. There is the great mass of the race; and there their instincts are less impaired by the infusion of alien blood and by hostile climatic influences. There we find the Negro in the almost unimpaired integrity of his race susceptibility, and he is by an uncontrollable impulse feeling after a congenial atmosphere which his nature tells him he can find only in Africa. And he is going to Africa.

As long as he remains in this country, he is hampered both in mind and body. He can conceive of no radiance, no beauty, no inspiration in what are ignorantly called "the Wilds of Africa." The society in which he lives in the lands of his exile he supposes, from knowing no other, to be the normal condition of man, and fancies that he will suffer if he leaves it. But when he gets home he finds the atmosphere there a part of himself. He puts off the garment which has hampered his growth here, and he finds that he not only does not take cold, but has a chance for healthful development.

There is not a single Negro in the United States on the road to practical truth, so far as his race is concerned. He feels something in him, his instincts point to it, but he cannot act out what he feels. And when he has made up his mind to remain in America, he has also made up his mind to surrender his race integrity; for he sees no chance of its preservation. There is in him neither hope enough to excite the desire to preserve it, nor desire enough to encourage the hope of its preservation. But, in Africa, he casts off his trammels. His wings develop, and he soars into an atmosphere of exhaustless truth for him. There he becomes a righteous man; he casts off his fears and his doubts. There for him is perpetual health; there he returns to reason and faith. There he feels that nothing can happen to the race. There he is surrounded by millions of men, as far as he can see or hear, just like himself, and he is delivered from the constant dread which harasses him in this country, as to what is to become of the Negro. There the solicitude is in the opposite direction. There he fears for the white man, living in a climate hostile, and often fatal to him.

But there are two other facts, not, perhaps, generally known, to which I would like to call attention. The first is, that, notwithstanding the thousands and millions who, by violence and plunder, have been taken from Africa, she is as populous to-day as she ever will be; and the other is, that Africa has never lost the better classes of her people. As a rule, those who were exported—nearly all the forty millions who have been brought away—belonged to the servile and criminal classes. Only here and there, by the accidents of war, or the misfortunes of politics, was a leading African brought away. Africa is often called the Niobe of the nations, in allusion to the fact that her children in such vast numbers have been torn from her bosom; but the analogy is not strictly accurate. The ancient fable tells that Niobe clung to her children with warding arms, while the envious deities shot child after child, daughters and fair sons, till the whole twelve were slain, and the mother, powerless to defend her off-spring, herself became a stone. Now this is not the fact with Africa. The children who were torn from her bosom she could well spare. She has not been petrified with grief; she has not become a stone. She is as prolific to-day as in the days of yore. Her greenness and fertility are perennial. It was said of her in the past, and it may be said of her to-day, that she is ever bringing forth something new.

And she has not been entirely bereaved even of those who have been torn from her bosom. In all the countries of their exile, severe as the ordeal has been, they have been preserved. It might be said of them as of the Hebrews in Egypt, "The more they afflicted them, the more they multiplied and grew."

No; if we are to gather an analogy to Africa from ancient fable, the Sphinx supplies us with a truer symbol. The Sphinx was said to sit in the road side, and put riddles to every passenger. If the man could not answer, she swallowed him alive. If he could solve the riddle, the Sphinx was slain. Has not Africa been, through the ages, sitting on the highway of the world? There she is, south of Europe, with but a lake between, joined on to Asia, with the most frequented oceans on the east and west of her—accessible to all the races, and yet her secret is unknown. She has swallowed up her thousands. The Sphinx must solve her own riddle at last. The opening up of Africa is to be the work of Africans.

In the Providence of God, it seems that this great and glorious work is reserved for the Negro. Centuries of effort and centuries of failure demonstrate that white men cannot build up colonies there. If we look at the most recent maps of Africa, we see that large tracts have been explored: English, German, Belgian, French, and American expeditions have lately described large portions of the continent; but every one must have been struck by the enormous gaps that remain to be filled in—the vast portions which the foot of the white man has never trodden. With the exception of the countries south of Egypt, the great lake region, and the strip of country from east to west, containing the routes of Cameron and Stanley, and if we leave out the portion of North Central Africa explored by Barth—the country is still as unknown to foreigners as it has been throughout all history, from the days of Herodotus and Ptolemy to the present. Who knows anything of the mountains of the moon? Of all that vast region which lies directly east of Liberia, as far as the Indian Ocean? What foreigner can tell anything of the interior of Bonny, or of Calabar? If we examine the

Continent, from the extreme south, from Egypt to Kaffraria or the country of the Zulus, we see very little yet accomplished. The most successful effort yet made in colonizing Africa is in Liberia. This will be permanent, because the colonists are of the indigenous stock. There are six hundred miles of coast, and two hundred miles of breadth, rescued for civilization. I mean, in that extent of country, over a million of people are on the road to self-elevation. They come in contact with an atmosphere of growth.

Now the people who are producing these changes have a peculiar claim upon this country—for they went out from this nation and are carrying American institutions into that Continent. And this great country has peculiar facilities for the work of African civilization. The nations of Europe are looking with anxious eyes to the "Dark Continent," as they love to call it, probably for the purpose of kindling their religious zeal, or stimulating their commercial instincts. But not one of them has the opportunity of entering that Continent with the advantages of the United States. They cannot send their citizens there from Europe to colonize—they die. France is now aiming at taking possession, by railroads, of the trade of Soudan, from Algeria and Senegal. But the success of the scheme, through European agency, is extremely problematical. The question has been mooted of transferring their Negro citizens from the West Indies—from Martinique and Guadaloupe—but they cannot spare them from those islands. England would like to transport to the countries of the Niger, and to the regions interior of Sierra Leone, civilized blacks from her colonies in the Western hemisphere; but to encourage such a movement would be to destroy Barbadoes, Jamaica, and Antigua. The King of the Belgians, in his philanthropic and commercial zeal for the opening and colonizing of Africa, has no population available. The United States is the only country which, providentially, can do the work which the whole world now wants done. Entering on the West Coast, through Liberia, she may stretch a chain of colonies of her own citizens through the whole length of the Soudan, from the Niger to the Nile—from the Atlantic to the Indian Ocean. "This country," said Dr. Storrs—

> has thousands of liberated and Christianized Africans in it, just at the moment when that dark continent is suddenly opened to the access of the Gospel. God has been building here a power, for the glory of His name, and for His service in the earth. I see the stamp held in the hand, and the liquid wax lying before it; and I do not doubt that the purpose is to fix the impression on

that wax from the engraved brass or stone. I see the men whom man has brought here, and whom God has converted, and before them those vast outstretching realms made ready for the truth; and I cannot doubt that His purpose is to fix by these men, upon those prepared lands, the inscription of the Gospel and the Cross! And it seems to me that in the end all men must feel this.

Some have already gone, the pioneers in this great work. Leaving the land of their birth, where they have laboured for generations, they have gone to brave the perils of another wilderness, to cut down forests, to clear away jungles, to make roads, to build towns, to cultivate farms, and to teach regular industry to their less favoured brethren; and they ask you to follow these new settlements, as they push into the heart of the continent, with all the aids and appliances of your advanced civilization.

In visions of the future, I behold those beautiful hills—the banks of those charming streams, the verdant plains and flowery fields, the salubrious highlands in primaeval innocence and glory, and those fertile districts watered everywhere as the garden of the Lord; I see them all taken possession of by the returning exiles from the West, trained for the work of re-building waste places under severe discipline and hard bondage. I see, too, their brethren hastening to welcome them from the slopes of the Niger, and from its lovely valleys—from many a sequestered nook, and from many a palmy plain—Mohammedans and Pagans, chiefs and people, all coming to catch something of the inspiration the exiles have brought—to share in the borrowed jewels they have imported, and to march back hand-in-hand with their returned brethren towards the sunrise for the regeneration of a continent. And under their united ages and rescued from a stagnant barbarism; and then to the astonishment of the whole world, in a higher sense than has yet been witnessed, "Ethiopia shall *suddenly* stretch out her hands unto God."

From the chapter entitled "African Colonization."

To the present generation of whites and blacks in America, it may seem that the Negro "is there to stay," but the next generation will take a different view. Descendants of Africa have never been permitted to feel at home in those countries, even where they are most numerous, and where the geographical and climatic conditions are congenial. Freedmen from Brazil and other parts of South America are continually making their way back to the Fatherland, anxious to breathe again the ancestral air, and to lie down at last, and be buried with their fathers.

In the United States, notwithstanding the great progress made in the direction of liberal ideas, the Negro is still a stranger. The rights and privileges accorded by constitutional law offer him no security against the decrees of private or social intolerance. He is surrounded by a prosperity—industrial, commercial, and political— in which he is not permitted to share, and is tantalized by social respectabilities from which he is debarred. The future offers no encouragement to him. In the career of courage and virtue, of honour, emolument, and fame, which lies open to his white neighbours, and to their children, neither he himself, nor his sons or daughters, can have any part. From that high and improving fellowship, which binds together the elements from Europe, however incongruous, the Negro child is excommunicated before he is born.

One fatal drawback to the Negro in America is the incubus of imitation. He must be an imitator; and imitators see only results— they never learn processes. They come in contact with accomplished facts, without knowing how they were accomplished. They never get within, so as to see how a thing originates or develops. Therefore, when they attempt anything, they are apt to begin at the end, without the insight, patience, or experience which teaches that they begin at the beginning. They are impatient theorists—in the literal sense—who can neither understand, nor wait for the slow results and precarious combinations of arduous and prolonged effort. Hence they are ready to criticize processes, to find fault with details. The destructive faculty is largely developed; but to originate, and point out methods of effective action, is impossible to them. John Jasper is a respectable Negro preacher of Virginia, who has constructed his own theory of the solar-system; and the fact that he has constructed something, and has the temerity to explain and defend his theory against the theories of the learned, causes a large following, and he has lately been invited to lecture in Europe as a curiosity. His earnestness and acuteness, in spite of his defiance of grammar, and his ignorance of scholastic methods, command the respect of the intelligent listener. It is easier to smile at his scientific perversity, than to give the reasoning by which the mighty results of astronomy have been obtained.

Whatever may be said of the advantages of education and civilization, and a great deal is being said just now, and, perhaps so far as the Negro is concerned, a great deal ought to be said—it seems certain that such advantages are not without serious dangers. It is our earnest belief that a real independent moral growth, productive of strength of character and self-reliance, is impossible to natures in contact with beings greatly superior to themselves. This is one reason, we suppose, why our spiritual training was not entrusted to angelic beings, why "we have this treasure in earthen vessels." Everybody knows that a powerful, massive character—though it be nearly perfect—may positively injure those within the circle of its influence by giving them a bent in a direction opposite to their own natural tendencies, so as to make it extremely difficult, if not impossible, for them to shake themselves free.

This is one of the great drawbacks to the introduction of civilization by foreigners into Africa. In the European settlements on the coast there are visible the melancholy effects of the fatal contagion of a mimic or spurious Europeanism. Some who have been to Europe bring back and diffuse among their people a reverence for some of the customs of that country, of which the more cultivated are trying to get rid. But, happily the inhospitable and inexorable climate prevents this pseudo-civilization, called "progress," from spreading to the interior. The tribes still retain their simplicity and remain unaffected. And may they remain so until they pass by normal and regular progress and natural steps to a higher plane on the line of their own race-development, when European habits and customs will be aimed at as accessories, rather than a principle of life.

But, besides the drawbacks in the learning of the schools, the educated Negro, in the United States, in the enjoyment of the advantages of culture, has come in contact, throughout the period of his training, with influences which warp him in the direction of self-depreciation, even more powerfully than the books which he reads, or the teachers to whom he listens. The instruction of the schools does, to a certain extent—perhaps to a great extent— improve, but it can neither reverse nor supersede the far more efficient education which comes from the experiences of daily life, which—

Week in, week out, from morn till night,

control and give direction to the mind.

Living as the wards of a people, who, out of their own *habitat*, instinctively dread deterioration—the loss of vitality and vigour— and who believe that their existence and growth depend upon constant self-assertion, as against all alien comers; and who, therefore, can neither give place nor opportunity to their former slaves, the Africans must be subjected to experiences which, in spite of the training received in the schools, must warp them out of the moral and intellectual perpendicular, and incline them to the attitude and practices of the creature who either climbs or crawls. Bishop H. M. Turner, of the African Methodist Episcopal Church, is constantly calling attention, in his outspoken and energetic style, to the disadvantages of the Negro in America; but nowhere has he given a more vivid presentation of the dreary and discouraging subject, than in a recent short article in the *Quarterly Review,* of his Church. To some, his picture will, perhaps, appear as a repulsive photograph. Still, he writes with a kindly indignation—with a deep and fervid earnestness, and a surprising humour and fun, that compel attention. He says:

> I need not repeat my well-known convictions as to the future of the race. I think our stay in this country is but temporary, at most. Nothing will remedy the evils of the Negro, but a great Christian nation upon the continent of Africa. White is God in this country, and black is the Devil. White is perfection, greatness, wisdom, industry, and all that is high and holy. Black is ignorance, degradation, indolence, and all that is low and vile; and three-fourths of the coloured people of the land do nothing day and night but cry: "Glory, honour, dominion, and greatness to White." Many of our so-called leading men are contaminated with the accursed disease or folly, as well as the thoughtless masses; and, as long as such a sentiment pervades the coloured race, the powers of Heaven cannot elevate him. No race of people can rise and manufacture better conditions while they hate and condemn themselves. A man must believe he is somebody, before he is acknowledged to be somebody. Hundreds of our most educated young men will put on as many airs over a position that requires them to dust the clothes of white men, as a superior man would over an appointment to the President's Cabinet. I deny that God himself could make a great man out of such a character, without a miracle—
> Mit Dummheit kämpfen Götter selbst vergebens.

The imagination of the Negro has been taken captive by his surroundings. His consciousness is not sufficiently disengaged to enable him to respect his own peculiarities. He can conceive of nothing different from his surroundings; and he does not wish to conceive of anything different, believing as he does that the ultima Thule of progress has been reached by the Anglo-Saxon. The Negro of the most powerful intellect must work by the pattern before him, and reproduce only what he has seen with his bodily eyes. The ideal faculty has not fair play, or any play at all. He is bound to endless imitation. If any original image is formed in his mind, it must be banished, or it is crowded out by the pressure of the actual. There is neither time nor opportunity to work it out. He must spend his days longing for the crumbs of social and political existence which fall from the white man's table:

> Simile ad nom che va di porta in porta
> Mendicando la vita.

There must be Africans in America who feel all this, who feel that they have a life of their own—a life destined to last; who protest against many things they see around them, even while they are bound to respect them. We are told that when Michelangelo looked at the lofty dome of the cathedral at Florence, he exclaimed, "I will not make one like you; I cannot make one better than you." There must be, among the seven millions, some, if not many, who share the proud humility of the great artist. To such, at times, there must come the tears of another artist: not, however, because they have exhausted their ideals, but from the conviction that there is no opportunity, the result would mean nothing amid incompatible and unsympathetic surroundings; that, like the monolith in Central Park, though fitted to beautify and adorn other scenes for thousands of years, the result of their conceptions, if not still-born, would rapidly crumble to decay under the action of an inhospitable and uncongenial climate. To such, there must be a longing for other scenes, where, forgetting the things that are behind, they may reach forward to things which promise vitality, usefulness, and prosperity to their race. But there are many, alas, who may never gain the fructifying atmosphere—who must always resemble those figures one sees in museums in Europe, which would be magnificent if they were complete; as they now stand, they are only splendid torsos—melancholy suggestions of unattainable possibilities.

MOJOLA AGBEBI

Mojola Agbebi was of Yoruba origin and a Christian from birth, his father having been a Christian "and a missionary labouring in the hinterland of Lagos when he was born," one account reads. Educated in England, Agbebi served as an editor for a Lagos newspaper for a while, but his career was essentially a religious one, with forays into West African politics. In 1911 he attended the First Universal Races Congress and read a paper on "The West African Problem" to the assemblage, which included Du Bois and Blyden. But it was his radical religious role which earns Agbebi credit for helping inspire his countrymen to an African consciousness.

The inaugural sermon he gave was, in effect, a denunciation of Christian hypocrisy and a demand that Christianity be cast in an African mold. The sermon had considerable impact in its own time, being reprinted in the *West African Mail,* the *Midland Herald,* and the *Methodist Weekly.* Editorial comment in the *Lagos Standard* and the *Sierra Leone Weekly News* was very enthusiastic. So was a letter written by Blyden from Sierra Leone on March 17, 1903: "Your remarkable discourse will, I believe, go a long way towards delivering the civilized African from these ridiculous incongruities, and making him understand and appreciate his place as an important spiritual force in the history of mankind."

Mojola Agbebi

From *Inaugural Sermon*

According to the Apostle's [Paul's] estimate, the preaching of Christ, the triumph of the Gospel, the success of practical righteousness is the essential thing, all others are non-essentials. Let us consider one or two of the non-essentials. Formularies are non-essentials. The prayers or prayer-books of certain Christians may not necessarily be the prayers or prayer-books of other Christians. With one people it might be considered suitable to use the sign of the cross, with others it may not. . . .

Hymn-books are non-essentials to the preaching of Jesus Christ. The hymns of one nation may not necessarily be those of another nation, and they may not be put in a book. The Christians of England may sing hymns different from the Christians of Armenia, of France, or of Africa, and one tribe may sing differently from another tribe. The grave Old Hundred, which may induce solemnity in Saint Paul's Cathedral, and the grand "Hallelujah Chorus," which has just been triumphantly rendered by your estimable choir, may both excite ridicule or disgust in a church among the Kroo. Tastes differ. English tunes and metres, English songs and hymns, some of them most unsuited to African aspiration and intelligence, have proved effective in weakening the talent for hymnology among African Christians. In one of the churches planted up-country, I have found it necessary to advise that for seven years, at least, no hymn-books but original hymns should be used at worship. African Christians dance to foreign music in their social festivities, they sing to foreign music in their funerals, and use foreign instruments to cultivate their musical aspirations. Throughout the entire scriptures there was not a case in which Christians sing foreign hymns, or an instance where

---

Source: Mojola Agbebi, "Inaugural Sermon Delivered at the Celebration of the First Anniversary of the 'African Church,'" Lagos, West Africa, December 21, 1902, pp. 5–10. From The Schomburg Collection of Negro Literature and History. By permission of The New York Public Library.

prayers were unanswered or worship unaccepted because hymns were not sung. We are come to the times when religious developments demand original songs and original tunes from the African Christian. . . . No one race or nation can fix the particular kind of tunes which will be universally conducive to worship. Tunes and songs depend on the frame of mind, the breadth of soul, the experience of life, the altitude of faith, and the latitude of love of the individual. . . . In the carrying out of the function of singing, therefore, let us always remember that we are Africans, and that we ought to sing African songs, and that in African style and fashion. . . .

The joys are one, Redemption is one, Christ is one, God is one, but our tongues are various and our styles innumerable. Hymn-books, therefore, are one of the non-essentials of worship. Prayer-books and hymn-books, harmonium-dedications, pew-constructions, surpliced choir, the white man's style, the white man's name, the white man's dress, are so many non-essentials, so many props and crutches affecting the religious manhood of the Christian African. Among the great essentials of religion are that the lame walk, the lepers are cleansed, the deaf hear, the dead are raised up, and the poor have the Gospel preached unto them. The Apostle James said: "Pure religion and undefiled before God and the Father is: 'To visit the fatherless and widows in their affliction and to keep one's self unspotted from the world.' " I would add, however, that at present the cultivation of cotton, the raising of rubber trees, of coffee, kola nuts, etc., the calling forth the riches of the soil, sanitation, and the promotion of handicrafts form part of the pressing essentials of religion. The African Moslem, our co-religionist, though he reads the Koran in Arabic and counts his beads as our Christian brother the Roman Catholic does, and though he repeats the same formula of prayer in an unknown tongue from mosques and minarets five times a day throughout Africa, yet he spreads no common prayer before him in his devotions and carries no hymn-book in his worship of the Almighty. His dress is after the manner of the Apostles and Prophets, and his name, though indicating his faith, was never put on in a way to denationalise or degrade him. Islam is the religion of Africa. Christianity lives here by suffrance. While Islam is a bloodless faith and an iconoclastic creed, Christianity has been derided by some of its European friends as a bloody faith, the doctrine of shambles and the executioner's creed. European Christianity is a dangerous thing. What do you think of a religion which holds a bottle of gin in one hand and a Common Prayer in another? Which carries a glass of rum as a *vade-mecum* to a "Holy" hymn-book. A religion which points with one hand to the skies, bidding you "lay up for yourselves treasures in heaven," and while you are looking up grasps all your worldly goods with the other hand, seizes your ancestral lands, labels your forests, and places your patrimony under inexplicable legislations? A religion which indulges in swine's flesh and yet cries, "Be ye holy, for I am holy." A religion which prays against "Those evils which the craft and subtlety of the devil or man worketh against us," and yet effects to deny incantation, charms or spells, and Satanism—a religion which arrogates to itself censorial functions on sexual morality, and yet promotes a dance, in which one man's wife dances in close contact, questionable proximity and improper attitude with another woman's husband. O! Christianity, what enormities are committed in thy name. Every day is making manifest our increasing difficulties with Islam. What shall we do with a faith which displays such alarming vitality and phenomenal adaptability among us? One of its most distressing aspects is that, while men, professedly Christian, European and African, high in "state of life," in condition of intellect, and rich in the graces of heart, have been found espousing the cause of Islam, and indirectly assisting to propagate its tenets, and to multiply and strengthen the number of its disciples, African Christianity has not had the like support of men belonging to another creed.

WILLIAM EDWARD BURGHARDT DU BOIS

Du Bois's life paralleled the century of black protest. Born in Great Barrington, Massachusetts, in 1868, he died in Ghana in 1963. During his long years, Du Bois championed the cause of the black in this country and the cause of the political redemption of Africa.

At an early age he exhibited a keen mind; his academic career led him from Fisk University to Harvard University and then to the University of Berlin. Armed with the usual academic titles, and with many scholarly distinctions in addition, he began his teaching career at Atlanta University, where he soon began editing the monumental Atlanta University series on the Negro in America. He founded *The Crisis* in 1910, a periodical which was to become one of the most distinguished black publications.

In his early life Du Bois believed in the possibilities of equal integration and therefore opposed the subordinate segregation proposed by Booker T. Washington and the Back-to-Africa movement sponsored by Marcus Garvey. But following upon the First World War, a trip to the Soviet Union, and the Depression, Du Bois became more and more disillusioned with the American capitalistic system and more sympathetic to the humanistic aspects of Marxist thought. Self-exiled, he died as an honored citizen of Ghana.

Du Bois is without question the most influential figure in the history of all black protest activities. Not only did he help found the National Association for the Advancement of Colored People (NAACP), but also he was the virtual leader and organizer—as well as the source of political inspiration—of the Pan-African movement, which he championed in the first years of the twentieth century and guided until the 1930's when domestic American problems arrested his attention.

A man of immense learning and sensitivity, with a prose style that was majestic, Du Bois was a prolific author. Among his outstanding works are *Suppression of the African Slave Trade* (1896), *The Negro* (1915), *Black Folk Then and Now* (1940), and *The World and Africa* (1946). None, however, has had the impact that *The Souls of Black Folk* (1903) has had here and abroad. A moving and profound excursion into the life and ethos of the American black, this book presents essays that forced the early reader to an appreciation "of the spiritual world in which ten thousand thousand Americans live and strive."

FURTHER READING: Francis Broderick. *W. E. B. Du Bois, Negro Leader in a Time of Crisis.* Stanford: Stanford University Press, 1955.

William Edward Burghardt Du Bois

From *The Souls of Black Folk*

After the Egyptian and Indian, the Greek and Roman, the Teuton and Mongolian, the Negro is a sort of seventh son, born with a veil, and gifted with second-sight in this American world—a world which yields him no true self-consciousness, but only lets him see himself through the revelation of the other world. It is a peculiar sensation, this double-consciousness, this sense of always looking at one's self through the eyes of others, of measuring one's soul by the tape of a world that looks on in amused contempt and pity. One ever feels his twoness—an American, a Negro; two souls, two thoughts, two unreconciled strivings; two warring ideals in one dark body, whose dogged strength alone keeps it from being torn asunder.

The history of the American Negro is the history of this strife—this longing to attain self-conscious manhood, to merge his double self into a better and truer self. In this merging he wishes neither of the older selves to be lost. He would not Africanize America, for America has too much to teach the world and Africa. He would not bleach his Negro soul in a flood of white Americanism, for he knows that Negro blood has a message for the world. He simply wishes to make it possible for a man to be both a Negro and an American, without being cursed and spit upon by his fellows, without having the doors of Opportunity closed roughly in his face.

This, then, is the end of his striving: to be a co-worker in the kingdom of culture, to escape both death and isolation, to husband and use his best powers and his latent genius. These powers of body and mind have in the past been strangely wasted, dispersed, or forgotten. The shadow of a mighty Negro past flits through the tale of Ethiopia the Shadowy and of Egypt the Sphinx. Throughout history, the powers of single black men flash here and there like falling stars, and die sometimes before the world has rightly gauged their

Source: W. E. B. Du Bois, *The Souls of Black Folk* (New York: Fawcett World Library, 1961), pp. 16–22. Reprinted exclusively by permission of Mrs. Shirley Graham Du Bois.

brightness. Here in America, in the few days since Emancipation, the black man's turning hither and thither in hesitant and doubtful striving has often made his very strength to lose effectiveness, to seem like absence of power, like weakness. And yet it is not weakness—it is the contradiction of double aims. The double-aimed struggle of the black artisan—on the one hand to escape white contempt for a nation of mere hewers of wood and drawers of water, and on the other hand to plough and nail and dig for a poverty-stricken horde—could only result in making him a poor craftsman, for he had but half a heart in either cause. By the poverty and ignorance of his people, the Negro minister or doctor was tempted toward quackery and demagogy; and by the criticism of the other world, toward ideals that made him ashamed of his lowly tasks. The would-be black *savant* was confronted by the paradox that the knowledge his people needed was a twice-told tale to his white neighbors, while the knowledge which would teach the white world was Greek to his own flesh and blood. The innate love of harmony and beauty that set the ruder souls of his people a-dancing and a-singing raised but confusion and doubt in the soul of the black artist; for the beauty revealed to him was the soul-beauty of a race which his larger audience despised, and he could not articulate the message of another people. This waste of double aims, this seeking to satisfy two unreconciled ideals, has wrought sad havoc with the courage and faith and deeds of ten thousand thousand people— has sent them often wooing false gods and invoking false means of salvation, and at times has even seemed about to make them ashamed of themselves.

Away back in the days of bondage they thought to see in one divine event the end of all doubt and disappointment; few men ever worshipped Freedom with half such unquestioning faith as did the American Negro for two centuries. To him, so far as he thought and dreamed, slavery was indeed the sum of all villainies, the cause of all sorrow, the root of all prejudice; Emancipation was the key to a promised land of sweeter beauty than ever stretched before the eyes of wearied Israelites. In song and exhortation swelled one refrain—Liberty; in his tears and curses the God he implored had Freedom in his right hand. At last it came—suddenly, fearfully, like a dream. With one wild carnival of blood and passion came the message in his own plaintive cadences:

> Shout, O children!
> Shout, you're free!
> For God has bought your liberty!

Years have passed away since then—ten, twenty, forty; forty years of national life, forty years of renewal and development, and yet the swarthy spectre sits in its accustomed seat at the Nation's feast. In vain do we cry to this our vastest social problem:

> Take any shape but that, and my firm nerves
> Shall never tremble!

The Nation has not yet found peace from its sins; the freedman has not yet found in freedom his promised land. Whatever of good may have come in these years of change, the shadow of a deep disappointment rests upon the Negro people—a disappointment all the more bitter because the unattained ideal was unbounded save by the simple ignorance of a lowly people.

The first decade was merely a prolongation of the vain search for freedom, the boon that seemed ever barely to elude their grasp—like a tantalizing will-o'-the-wisp, maddening and misleading the headless host. The holocaust of war, the terrors of the Ku Klux Klan, the lies of carpet-baggers, the disorganization of industry, and the contradictory advice of friends and foes, left the bewildered serf with no new watchword beyond the old cry for freedom. As the time flew, however, he began to grasp a new idea. The ideal of liberty demanded for its attainment powerful means, and these the Fifteenth Amendment gave him. The ballot, which before he had looked upon as a visible sign of freedom, he now regarded as the chief means of gaining and perfecting the liberty with which war had partially endowed him. And why not? Had not votes made war and emancipated millions? Had not votes enfranchised the freedmen? Was anything impossible to a power that had done all this? A million black men started with renewed zeal to vote themselves into the kingdom. So the decade flew away, the revolution of 1876 came, and left the half-free serf weary, wondering, but still inspired. Slowly but steadily, in the following years, a new vision began gradually to replace the dream of political power—a powerful movement, the rise of another ideal to guide the unguided, another pillar of fire by night after a clouded day. It was the ideal of "book-learning"; the curiosity, born of compulsory ignorance, to know and test the power of the cabalistic letters of the white man, the longing to know. Here at last seemed to have been discovered the mountain path to Canaan; longer than the highway of Emancipation and law, steep and rugged, but straight, leading to heights high enough to overlook life.

Up the new path the advance guard toiled, slowly, heavily, doggedly; only those who have watched and guided the faltering feet, the misty minds, the dull understandings, of the dark pupils of these schools know how faithfully, how piteously, this people strove to learn. It was weary work. The cold statistician wrote down the inches of progress here and there, noted also where here and there a foot had slipped or some one had fallen. To the tired climbers, the horizon was ever dark, the mists were often cold, the Canaan was always dim and far away. If, however, the vistas disclosed as yet no goal, no resting-place, little but flattery and criticism, the journey at least gave leisure for reflection and self-examination; it changed the child of Emancipation to the youth with dawning self-consciousness, self-realization, self-respect. In those sombre forests of his striving his own soul rose before him, and he saw himself—darkly as through a veil; and yet he saw in himself some faint revelation of his power, of his mission. He began to have a dim feeling that, to attain his place in the world, he must be himself, and not another. For the first time he sought to analyze the burden he bore upon his back, that dead-weight of social degradation partially masked behind a half-named Negro problem. He felt his poverty; without a cent, without a home, without land, tools, or savings, he had entered into competition with rich, landed, skilled neighbors. To be a poor man is hard, but to be a poor race in a land of dollars is the very bottom of hardships. He felt the weight of his ignorance—not simply of letters, but of life, of business, of the humanities; the accumulated sloth and shirking and awkwardness of decades and centuries shackled his hands and feet. Nor was his burden all poverty and ignorance. The red stain of bastardy, which two centuries of systematic legal defilement of Negro women had stamped upon his race, meant not only the loss of ancient African chastity, but also the hereditary weight of a mass of corruption from white adulterers, threatening almost the obliteration of the Negro home.

A people thus handicapped ought not to be asked to race with the world, but rather allowed to give all its time and thought to its own social problems. But alas! while sociologists gleefully count his bastards and his prostitutes, the very soul of the toiling, sweating black man is darkened by the shadow of a vast despair. Men call the shadow prejudice, and learnedly explain it as the natural defence of culture against barbarism, learning against ignorance, purity against crime, the "higher" against the "lower" races. To which the Negro cries Amen! and swears that to so much of this strange prejudice as is founded on just homage to civilization, culture, righteousness, and progress, he humbly bows and meekly does obeisance. But before that nameless prejudice that leaps beyond all this he stands helpless, dismayed, and well-nigh speechless; before that personal disrespect and mockery, the ridicule and systematic humiliation, the distortion of fact and wanton license of fancy, the cynical ignoring of the better and the boisterous welcoming of the worse, the all-pervading desire to inculcate disdain for everything black, from Toussaint to the devil —before this there rises a sickening despair that would disarm and discourage any nation save that black host to whom "discouragement" is an unwritten word.

But the facing of so vast a prejudice could not but bring the inevitable self-questioning, self-disparagement, and lowering of ideals which ever accompany repression and breed in an atmosphere of contempt and hate. Whisperings and portents came borne upon the four winds: Lo! we are diseased and dying, cried the dark hosts; we cannot write, our voting is vain; what need of education, since we must always cook and serve? And the Nation echoed and enforced this self-criticism, saying: Be content to be servants, and nothing more; what need of higher culture for half-men? Away with the black man's ballot, by force or fraud—and behold the suicide of a race! Nevertheless, out of the evil came something of good—the more careful adjustment of education to real life, the clearer perception of the Negroes' social responsibilities, and the sobering realization of the meaning of progress.

So dawned the time of *Sturm und Drang*: storm and stress to-day rocks our little boat on the mad waters of the world-sea; there is within and without the sound of conflict, the burning of body and rending of soul; inspiration strives with doubt, and faith with vain questionings. The bright ideals of the past—physical freedom, political power, the training of brains and the training of hands—all these in turn have waxed and waned, until even the last grows dim and overcast. Are they all wrong—all false? No, not that, but each alone was over-simple and incomplete—the dreams of a credulous race-childhood, or the fond imaginings of the other world which does not know and does not want to know our power. To be really true, all these ideals must be melted and welded into one. The training of the schools we need to-day more than ever—the training of deft hands quick eyes and ears, and above all the broader, deeper, higher culture of gifted minds and pure hearts. The power of the ballot we need in sheer self-defence—else what shall save us from a second slavery? Freedom, too, long-sought, we still seek—the freedom of life and limb, the freedom to work and think, the freedom to love and aspire

Work, culture, liberty—all these we need, not singly but together, not successively but together, each growing and aiding each, and all striving toward that vaster ideal that swims before the Negro people, the ideal of human brotherhood, gained through the unifying ideal of Race; the ideal of fostering and developing the traits and talents of the Negro, not in opposition to or contempt for other races, but rather in large conformity to the greater ideals of the American Republic, in order that some day on American soil two world-races may give each to each those characteristics both so sadly lack. We the darker ones come even now not altogether empty-handed: there are to-day no truer exponents of the pure human spirit of the Declaration of Independence than the American Negroes; there is no true American music but the wild sweet melodies of the Negro slave; the American fairy tales and folk-lore are Indian and African; and, all in all, we black men seem the sole oasis of simple faith and reverence in a dusty desert of dollars and smartness. Will America be poorer if she replace her brutal dyspeptic blundering with light-hearted but determined Negro humility? or her coarse and cruel wit with loving jovial good-humor? or her vulgar music with the soul of the Sorrow Songs?

Merely a concrete test of the underlying principles of the great republic is the Negro Problem, and the spiritual striving of the freedmen's sons is the travail of souls whose burden is almost beyond the measure of their strength, but who bear it in the name of an historic race, in the name of this the land of their fathers' fathers, and in the name of human opportunity.

J. E. CASELY HAYFORD

Casely Hayford was born in 1886 in the Gold Coast and received his early education at Fourah Bay College in Sierra Leone. After a short period as principal of an Accra high school, he went to Cambridge to study the law. His return to the Gold Coast was soon followed by his involvement in land issues and native rights which, in turn, aroused his concern over the plight of his people under colonial rule. Influenced by Blyden, he began to stress those qualities of spirituality and commonalty which he believed to be characteristic of the African. As he became a significant leader of thought and political action in West Africa, he emphasized the need for West African unity and was responsible for a National Congress of British West Africa, which met in Accra in 1920. This latter event, suggestive of an intensifying Pan-Africanism, was in a way the peak of Casely Hayford's career, and the occasion for his clarion call to African unity through self-determination. Casely Hayford, like Blyden before him and Senghor after him, had a mystical view of Africa and anticipated a future role in which the continent would help regenerate the world, much as Mazzini had hoped Italy would do a century before. Casely Hayford saw Africa as "the cradle of the world's systems and philosophies, and the nursing mother of its religions."

Ethiopia Unbound is in plot concerned with the cultural excursion of Kwamankra, a British-educated native of the Gold Coast who stands strongly for his country and her past but is also imbued with many of the values derived from a Western education. The novel is essentially a vehicle for Casely Hayford's political and cultural views. Kwamankra's hero is Blyden. As Kwamankra remarked in a speech he gave at Hampton Institute in 1907: "The work of men like Booker T. Washington and W. E. Burghardt Du Bois is exclusive and provincial. The work of Edward Wilmot Blyden is universal, covering the entire race and the entire race problem." That *Ethiopia Unbound* is dedicated to the "Sons of Ethiopia the World Wide Over" suggests Casely Hayford's own broad view of black culture.

FURTHER READING: Robert July. *The Origins of Modern African Thought.* New York: Frederick A. Praeger, Inc., 1967. See Chapter 21: "The Metamorphosis of Casely Hayford."

J. E. Casely Hayford

From *Ethiopia Unbound:*
Studies in Race Emancipation

In the name of African nationality the thinker would, through the medium of *Ethiopia Unbound,* greet members of the race everywhere throughout the world. Whether in the east, south, or west of the African Continent, or yet among the teeming millions of Ethiopia's sons in America, the cry of the African, in its last analysis, is for scope and freedom in the struggle for existence, and it would seem as if the care of the leaders of the race has been to discover those avenues of right and natural endeavor which would, in the end, ensure for the race due recognition of its individuality.

The race problem is probably most intense in the United States of America, but there are indications that on the African Continent itself it is fast assuming concrete form. Sir Arthur Lawley, the present Governor of Madras, before leaving the Governorship of the Transvaal, is reported in a public address to have said that the "black peril" is a reality, and to have advised the whites to consolidate their forces in the presence of the potential foe. The leaders of the race have hitherto exercised sound discretion and shown considerable wisdom in advising the African to follow the line of least resistance in meeting any combination of forces against him. The African's way to proper recognition lies not at present so much in the exhibition of material force and power, as in the gentler art of persuasion by the logic of facts and of achievements before which all reasonable men must bow.

A two-fold danger threatens the African everywhere. It is the outcome of certain economic conditions whose method is the exploitation of the Ethiopian for all he is worth. He is said to be

Source: J. E. Casely Hayford, *Ethiopia Unbound: Studies in Race Emancipation* (London: C. Phillips, 1911), pp. 167–177.

pressed into the service of man, in reality, the service of the Caucasian. That being so, he never reaps the full meed of his work as a *man*. He materially contributes to the building of pavements on which he may not walk—take it as a metaphor, or as a fact, which way you please. He hopes to work up revenues and to fill up exchequers over which, in most cases, he has no effective control, if any at all. In brief, he is labelled as belonging to a class apart among the races, and any attempt to rise above his station is terribly resented by the aristocracy of the races. Indeed, he is reminded at every turn that he is only intended to be a hewer of wood and a drawer of water. And so it happens that those among the favoured sons of men who occasionally consider the lot of the Ethiopian are met with jeers and taunts. Is it any wonder, then, that even in the Twentieth Century, the African finds it terribly difficult to make headway even in his own country? The African may turn socialist, may preach and cry for reform until the day of Judgment; but the experience of mankind shows this, that reform never comes to a class or a people unless and until those concerned have worked out their own salvation. And the lesson we have yet to learn is that we cannot depart from Nature's way and hope for real success.

And yet, it would seem as if in some notable instances the black man is bent upon following the line of greatest resistance in coping with the difficulties before him. Knowledge is the common property of mankind, and the philosophy which seeks for the Ethiopian the highest culture and efficiency in industrial and technical training is a sound one. It is well to arrest in favour of the race public opinion as to its capability in this direction. But that is not all, since there are certain distinctive qualities of race, of country, and of peoples which cannot be ignored without detriment to the particular race, country, or people. Knowledge, deprived of the assimilating element which makes it natural to the one taught, renders that person but a bare imitator. The Japanese, adopting and assimilating Western culture, of necessity commands the respect of Western nations, because there is something distinctly Eastern about him. He commands, to begin with, the uses of his native tongue, and has a literature of his own, enriched by translations from standard authors of other lands. He respects the institutions and customs of his ancestors, and there is an intelligent past which inspires him. He does not discard his national costume, and if, now and again, he dons Western attire, he does so as a matter of convenience, much as the Scotch, across the border, puts away, when the occasion demands it, his Highland costume. It is not the fault of the black man in America, for example, that he suffers to-day from the effects of a wrong that was inflicted upon him years ago by the forefathers of the very ones who now despise him. But he can see to it that as the years go by it becomes a matter of necessity for the American whites to respect and admire his manhood; and the surest way to the one or the other lies not so much in imitation as in originality and natural initiative. Not only must the Ethiopian acquire proficiency in the arts and sciences, in technical and industrial training, but he must pursue a course of scientific enquiry which would reveal to him the good things of the treasure house of his own nationality.

There are probably but a few men of African descent in America who, if they took the trouble by dipping into family tradition, would not be able to trace their connection and relationship with one or other of the great tribes of West Africa; and now that careful enquiry has shown that the institutions of the Aborigines of Africa are capable of scientific handling, what would be easier than for the great centres of culture and learning in the hands of Africans in the United States to found professorships in this relation? In the order of Providence, some of our brethren aforetime were suffered to be enslaved in America for a wise purpose. That event in the history of the race has made it possible for the speedier dissemination and adoption of the better part of Western culture; and to-day Africa's sons in the East and in the West can do peculiar service unto one another in the common cause of uplifting Ethiopia and placing her upon her feet among the nations. The East, for example, can take lessons from the West in the adoption of a sound educational policy, the kind of industrial and technical training which would enable aboriginals to make the best use of their lands and natural resources. And, surely, the West ought not to be averse to taking hints from the East as regards the preservation of national institutions, and the adoption of distinctive garbs and names, much as obtains among our friends the Japanese. While a student in London, a thrill of Oriental pride used to run through the writer when he brushed against an Asiatic in a garb distinctively Eastern. They aped no one. They were content to remain Eastern. For even when climatic conditions necessitated the adoption of European habiliments, they had sense enough to preserve some symbol of nationality. On the contrary, Africans would seem never to be content unless and until they make it possible for the European to write of them thus:

> How extraordinary is the spectacle of this huge race—millions of men—without land or language of their own, without tradi-

tions of the country they came from, bearing the very names of the men that enslaved them! . . .

The black element is one which cannot be "boiled down" into the great cosmopolitan American nation—the black man must always be tragically apart from the white man—

and so on and so forth.

Now, if there is aught in the foregoing which is true to life, it bears but one meaning, namely, this, that the average Afro-American citizen of the United States has lost absolute touch with the past of his race, and is helplessly and hopelessly groping in the dark for affinities that are not natural, and for effects for which there are neither national nor natural causes. That being so, the African in America is in a worse plight than the Hebrew in Egypt. The one preserved his language, his manners and customs, his religion and household gods; the other has committed national suicide, and at present it seems as if the dry bones of the vision have no life in them. Looking at the matter closely, it is not so much *Afro-Americans* that we want as *Africans* or *Ethiopians,* sojourning in a strange land, who, out of a full heart and a full knowledge can say: If I forget thee, Ethiopia, let my right hand forget its cunning! Let us look at the other side of the picture. How extraordinary would be the spectacle of this huge Ethiopian race—some millions of men—having imbibed all that is best in Western culture in the land of their oppressors, yet remaining true to racial instincts and inspiration, customs and institutions, much as did the Israelites of old in captivity! When this more pleasant picture will have become possible of realisation, then, and only then, will it be possible for our people in bondage "metaphorically to walk out of Egypt in the near future with a great and a real spoil."

Someone may say, but, surely, you don't mean to suggest that questions of dress and habits of life matter in the least. I reply emphatically, they do. They go to the root of the Ethiopian's self-respect. Without servile imitation of our teachers in their get-up and manner of life, it stands to reason that the average white man would regard the average black man far more seriously than he does at present. The adoption of a distinctive dress for the cultured African, therefore, would be a distinct step forward, and a gain to the cause of Ethiopian progress and advancement. Pray listen to the greatest authority on national life upon this matter:

> Behold, I have taught you statutes and judgments even as the Lord God commanded me that ye should do in the land whither

ye go to possess it. Keep, therefore, and do them: for this is your wisdom and your understanding in the sight of the nations which shall hear these statutes and say, surely, this great nation is a wise and understanding people.

Yes, my people are pursuing knowledge as for a hidden treasure, and have neglected wisdom and true understanding, and hence are they daily a laughing stock in the sight of the nations.

Here, then, is work for cultured West Africans to start a reform which will be world-wide in its effects among Ethiopians, remembering as a basis that we, as a people, have our own statutes, the customs and institutions of our fore-fathers, which we cannot neglect and live. We on the Gold Coast are making a huge effort in this direction, and though European habits will die hard with some of our people, the effort is worth making; and, if we don't succeed quite with this generation, we shall succeed with the next. That the movement is gaining ground may well be gathered from the following extract from the *Gold Coast Leader of* 24th February, 1907, reporting the coronation of Ababio IV, *Mantse,* that is King, of "British Accra." Says the correspondent:

> For the first time I realized that the Gold Coast would be more exhilarating and enjoyable indeed if the educated inhabitants in it would hark back to the times of old and take a few lessons in the art and grace of the sartorial simplicity and elegance of their forebears. The "scholars" looked quite noble and full of dignity in the native dress. There was not one ignoble or mean person among them, and so for the matter of that did the ladies.

Then I should like to see *Ethiopian Leagues* formed throughout the United States much in the same way as the *Gaelic League* in Ireland, for the purpose of studying and employing Fanti, Yoruba, Hausa, or other standard African language, in daily use. The idea may seem extraordinary on the first view, but if you are inclined to regard it thus, I can only point to the examples of Ireland and Denmark, who have found the vehicle of a national language much the safest and most natural way of national conservancy and evolution. If the Dane and Irish find it expedient in Europe, surely the matter is worthy of consideration by the Ethiopian in the United States, in Sierra Leone, in the West Indies, and in Liberia.

A distinguished writer, dwelling upon the advantages of culture in a people's own language said:

These are important considerations of a highly practical kind. Ten years ago, we had in Ireland a people divorced, by half a century of education conducted along alien lines, from their own proper language and culture. We had also in Ireland a people seemingly incapable of rational action, sunk in hopeless poverty, apparently doomed to disappear. We have in Ireland to-day the beginnings of a system of education in the national language and along national lines; and we have at the same time, and in the places where this kind of education has been operative, an unmistakable advance in intellectual capacity and material prosperity.

Now, if the soul that is in the Ethiopian, even in the United States, remains Ethiopian, which it does, to judge from the coon songs which have enriched the sentiment of mankind by their pathos, then, I say, the foregoing words, true as everyone must admit they are, point distinctly to the impossibility of departing from *nature's* way with any hope of lasting good to African nationality. I do sincerely trust these thoughts will catch the eye of such distinguished educationists as Mr. Booker T. Washington and others of the United States and in the West Indies as also the attention of similar workers in West Africa who have the materials ready at hand. It is a great work, but I do believe that my countrymen have the heart and the intelligence to grapple with it successfully.

MARCUS AURELIUS GARVEY

Marcus Garvey, born in Jamaica in 1887, was largely a self-educated man who began a career as a printer. Travels and employment in Central and South America, notably a stint as a worker for the United Fruit Company, made him aware of the unequal and severe treatment accorded to the black West Indian and convinced him of the need for concerted political action. After a visit to England in 1912, where he became acquainted with the then incipient Pan-African movement, he immersed himself in readings on Africa. Upon his return to Jamaica, he founded the Universal Negro Improvement Association (UNIA). In correspondence with Booker T. Washington, Garvey was invited by him to come to Tuskegee; but Garvey arrived in the United States in 1916, shortly after Washington's death. He then settled in New York and began the extensive and elaborate activities that made him a figure of great attention and significance. A believer in black capitalism, he founded the Black Star Steamship Line, an expensive and financially foolish venture, and the Negro Factory Corporation. As self-proclaimed Provisional President of the Republic of Africa, he invested himself and his followers with titles and offices, and ardently preached the Back-to-Africa idea.

This activity was greeted with less than universal enthusiasm; Garvey unhappily acquired a large number of detractors and opponents, who were not distressed when he was jailed in 1922 on charges of fraud. Released from jail in 1927 by way of a presidential commutation, Garvey was deported as an undesirable alien to Jamaica. He went to England sometime later and there died a forgotten and broken man in 1940.

Philosophy and Opinions of Marcus Garvey is a compilation made by Garvey's wife, Amy Jacques Garvey, in 1923, of Garvey's most important writings, speeches, and epigrams. As an anthology, it is striking in its constancy: the themes of racial separatism, black emigration from the USA to Africa, black power, and the political redemption of Africa occur over and over again.

A testimony to the significance of Garvey's work was provided by Kwame Nkrumah, founding president of Ghana and one of Africa's most important ideologues: "I think that of all the literature that I have studied, the book that did more than any other to fire my enthusiasm was the *Philosophy and Opinions of Marcus Garvey*."

FURTHER READING: Edward D. Cronin. *Black Moses: The Story of Marcus Garvey and the Universal Negro Improvement Association.* Madison: University of Wisconsin Press, 1955.

Marcus Aurelius Garvey

From *Philosophy and Opinions of Marcus Garvey*

From "An Appeal to the Soul of White America," written on October 2, 1923.

Surely the soul of liberal, philanthropic, liberty-loving, white America is not dead.

It is true that the glamor of materialism has, to a great degree, destroyed the innocence and purity of the national conscience, but, still, beyond our politics, beyond our soulless industrialism, there is a deep feeling of human sympathy that touches the soul of white America, upon which the unfortunate and sorrowful can always depend for sympathy, help, and action.

It is to that feeling that I appeal for four hundred million Negroes of the world, and fifteen millions of America in particular.

There is no real white man in America, who does not desire a solution of the Negro problem. Each thoughtful citizen has probably his own idea of how the vexed question of races should be settled. To some the Negro could be gotten rid of by wholesale butchery, by lynching, by economic starvation, by a return to slavery, and legalized oppression, while others would have the problem solved by seeing the race all herded together and kept somewhere among themselves; but a few—those in whom they have an interest—should be allowed to live around as the wards of a mistaken philanthropy; yet, none so generous as to desire to see the Negro elevated to a standard of real progress and prosperity, welded into a homogeneous whole, creating of themselves a mighty nation, with proper systems of government, civilization, and culture, to mark them admissible to the fraternities of nations and races without any disadvantage.

I do not desire to offend the finer feelings and sensibilities of those

---

Source: *Philosophy and Opinions of Marcus Garvey,* reprinted by permission of the publishers, Frank Cass and Co. Limited, London, 1967, pp. 1–6, 22–26.

white friends of the race who really believe that they are kind and considerate to us as a people; but I feel it my duty to make a real appeal to conscience and not to belief. Conscience is solid, convicting, and permanently demonstrative; belief is only a matter of opinion, changeable by superior reasoning. Once the belief was that it was fit and proper to hold the Negro as a slave, and in this the bishop, priest, and layman agreed. Later on, they changed their belief or opinion, but at all times, the conscience of certain people dictated to them that it was wrong and inhuman to hold human beings as slaves. It is to such a conscience in white America that I am addressing myself.

Negroes are human beings—the peculiar and strange opinions of writers, ethnologists, philosophers, scientists, and anthropologists notwithstanding. They have feelings, souls, passions, ambitions, desires, just as other men; hence they must be considered.

Has white America really considered the Negro in the light of permanent human progress? The answer is NO.

Men and women of the white race, do you know what is going to happen if you do not think and act now? One of two things. You are either going to deceive and keep the Negro in your midst until you have perfectly completed your wonderful American civilization with its progress of art, science, industry, and politics, and then, jealous of your own success and achievements in those directions, and with the greater jealousy of seeing your race pure and unmixed, cast him off to die in the whirlpool of economic starvation, thus getting rid of another race that was not intelligent enough to live, or, you simply mean by the largeness of your hearts to assimilate fifteen million Negroes into the social fraternity of an American race, that will neither be white nor black! Don't be alarmed! We must prevent both consequences. No real race-loving white man wants to destroy the purity of his race, and no real Negro conscious of himself, wants to die, hence there is room for an understanding, and an adjustment. And that is just what we seek.

Let white and black stop deceiving themselves. Let the white race stop thinking that all black men are dogs and not to be considered as human beings. Let foolish Negro agitators and so-called reformers, encouraged by deceptive or unthinking white associates, stop preaching and advocating the doctrine of "social equality," meaning thereby the social intermingling of both races, intermarriages, and general social co-relationship. The two extremes will get us nowhere, other than breeding hate, and encouraging discord, which will eventually end disastrously to the weaker race.

Some Negroes, in the quest of position and honor, have been admitted to the full enjoyment of their constitutional rights. Thus we have some of our men filling high and responsible government positions, others, on their own account, have established themselves in the professions, commerce, and industry. This, the casual onlooker, and even the men themselves, will say carries a guarantee and hope of social equality, and permanent racial progress. But this is the mistake. There is no progress of the Negro in America that is permanent, so long as we have with us the monster evil—prejudice.

Prejudice we shall always have between black and white, so long as the latter believes that the former is intruding upon their rights. So long as white laborers believe that black laborers are taking and holding their jobs; so long as white artisans believe that black artisans are performing the work that they should do; so long as white men and women believe that black men and women are filling the positions that they covet; so long as white political leaders and statesmen believe that black politicians and statesmen are seeking the same positions in the nation's government; so long as white men believe that black men want to associate with, and marry white women, then we will ever have prejudice, and not only prejudice, but riots, lynchings, burnings, and God to tell what next will follow!

It is this danger that drives me mad. It must be prevented. We cannot allow white and black to drift along unthinkingly toward this great gulf and danger, that is nationally ahead of us. It is because of this that I speak, and now call upon the soul of great white America to help.

It is no use putting off. The work must be done, and it must be started now.

Some people have misunderstood me. Some don't want to understand me. But I must explain myself for the good of the world and humanity.

Those of the Negro race who preach social equality, and who are working for an American race that will, in complexion, be neither white nor black, have tried to misinterpret me to the white public, and create prejudice against my work. The white public, not stopping to analyze and question the motive behind criticisms and attacks aimed against new leaders and their movements, condemn without giving a chance to the criticised, to be heard. Those of my own race who oppose me because I refuse to endorse their program of social arrogance and social equality, gloat over the fact that by their misrepresentation and underhand methods, they were able to have me convicted and imprisoned for crime which they calculate will so discredit me as to destroy the movement that I represent, in opposition to their program of a new American race; but we will not now consider the opposition to a program or a movement, but state the facts as they are, and let deep souled white America pass its own judgment.

In another one hundred years white America will have doubled its population; in another two hundred years it will have trebled itself. The keen student must realize that the centuries ahead will bring us an over-crowded country; opportunities, as the population grows larger, will be fewer; the competition for bread between the people of their own class will become keener, and so much more so will there be no room for two competitive races, the one strong, and the other weak. To imagine Negroes as district attorneys, judges, senators, congressmen, and laborers at work, while millions of white men starve, is to have before you the bloody picture of wholesale mob violence that I fear, and against which I am working.

No preaching, no praying, no presidential edict will control the passion of hungry unreasoning men of prejudice when the hour comes. It will not come, I pray, in our generation, but it is of the future that I think and for which I work.

A generation of ambitious Negro men and women, out from the best colleges, universities, and institutions, capable of filling the highest and best positions in the nation, in industry, commerce, society, and politics! Can you keep them back? If you do so they will agitate and throw your Constitution in your faces. Can you stand before civilization and deny the truth of your Constitution? What are you going to do then? You who are just will open the door of opportunity and say to all and sundry, "Enter in." But, ladies and gentlemen, what about the mob, that starving crowd of your own race? Will they stand by, suffer and starve, and allow an opposite, competitive race to prosper in the midst of their distress? If you can conjure these things up in your mind, then you have the vision of the race problem of the future in America.

There is but one solution and that is to provide an outlet for Negro energy, ambition, and passion, away from the attractions of white opportunity, and surround the race with opportunities of its own. If this is not done, and if the foundation for same is not laid now, then the consequence will be sorrowful for the weaker race, and disgraceful to our ideals of justice, and shocking to our civilization.

The Negro must have a country and a nation of his own. If you laugh at the idea, then you are selfish and wicked, for you and your children do not intend that the Negro shall discommode you in yours. If you do not want him to have a country and a nation of his own; if you do not intend to give him equal opportunities in yours, then it is plain to see that you mean that he must die, even as the Indian, to make room for your generations.

Why should the Negro die? Has he not served America and the world? Has he not borne the burden of civilization in this Western world for three hundred years? Has he not contributed of his best to America? Surely all this stands to his credit. But there will not be enough room and the one answer is "find a place." We have found a place; it is Africa, and as black men for three centuries have helped white men build America, surely generous and grateful white men will help black men build Africa.

And why shouldn't Africa and America travel down the ages as protectors of human rights and guardians of democracy? Why shouldn't black men help white men secure and establish universal peace? We can only have peace when we are just to all mankind; and for that peace, and for the reign of universal love, I now appeal to the soul of white America. Let the Negroes have a government of their own. Don't encourage them to believe that they will become social equals and leaders of the whites in America, without first on their own account proving to the world that they are capable of evolving a civilization of their own. The white race can best help the Negro by telling him the truth and not by flattering him into believing that he is as good as any white man without first proving the racial, national, constructive metal of which he is made.

Stop flattering the Negro about social equality, and tell him to go to work and build for himself. Help him in the direction of doing for himself, and let him know that self-progress brings its own reward.

I appeal to the considerate and thoughtful conscience of white America not to condemn the cry of the Universal Negro Improvement Association for a nation in Africa for Negroes, but to give us a chance to explain ourselves to the world. White America is too big, and when informed and touched, too liberal, to turn down the cry of the awakened Negro for "a place in the sun."

From "An Appeal to the Conscience of the Black Race to See Itself."

It is said to be a hard and difficult task to organize and keep together large numbers of the Negro race for the common good. Many have tried to congregate us, but have failed, the reason being that our characteristics are such as to keep us more apart than together.

The evil of internal division is wrecking our existence as a people, and if we do not seriously and quickly move in the direction of a readjustment it simply means that our doom becomes imminently conclusive.

For years the Universal Negro Improvement Association has been working for the unification of our race, not on domestic-national lines only, but universally. The success which we have met in the course of our effort is rather encouraging, considering the time consumed and the environment surrounding the object of our concern.

It seems that the whole world of sentiment is against the Negro, and the difficulty of our generation is to extricate ourselves from the prejudice that hides itself beneath, as well as above, the action of an international environment.

Prejudice is conditional on many reasons, and it is apparent that the Negro supplies, consciously or unconsciously, all the reasons by which the world seems to ignore and avoid him. No one cares for a leper, for lepers are infectious persons, and all are afraid of the disease, so, because the Negro keeps himself poor, helpless and undemonstrative, it is natural also that no one wants to be of him or with him.

Progress is the attraction that moves humanity, and to whatever people or race this "modern virtue" attaches itself, there will you find the splendor of pride and self-esteem that never fail to win the respect and admiration of all.

It is the progress of the Anglo-Saxons that singles them out for the respect of all the world. When their race had no progress or achievement to its credit, then, like all other inferior peoples, they paid the price in slavery, bondage, as well as through prejudice. We cannot forget the time when even the ancient Briton was regarded as being too dull to make a good Roman slave, yet today the influence of that race rules the world.

It is the industrial and commercial progress of America that causes Europe and the rest of the world to think appreciatively of the Anglo-American race. It is not because one hundred and ten million people live in the United States that the world is attracted to the republic with so much reverence and respect—a reverence and respect not shown to India with its three hundred millions, or to China with its four hundred millions. Progress of and among any people will advance them in the respect and appreciation of the rest of their fellows. It is such a progress that the Negro must attach to himself if he is to rise above the prejudice of the world.

The reliance of our race upon the progress and achievements of others for a consideration in sympathy, justice, and rights is like a dependence upon a broken stick, resting upon which will eventually consign you to the ground.

The Universal Negro Improvement Association teaches our race self-help and self-reliance, not only in one essential, but in all those things that contribute to human happiness and well-being. The disposition of the many to depend upon the other races for a kindly and sympathetic consideration of their needs, without making the effort to do for themselves, has been the race's standing disgrace by which we have been judged and through which we have created the strongest prejudice against ourselves.

There is no force like success, and that is why the individual makes all efforts to surround himself throughout life with the evidence of it. As of the individual, so should it be of the race and nation. The glittering success of Rockefeller makes him a power in the American nation; the success of Henry Ford suggests him as an object of universal respect, but no one knows and cares about the bum or hobo who is Rockefeller's or Ford's neighbor. So, also, is the world attracted by the glittering success of races and nations, and pays absolutely no attention to the bum or hobo race that lingers by the wayside.

The Negro must be up and doing if he will break down the prejudice of the rest of the world. Prayer alone is not going to improve our condition, nor the policy of watchful waiting. We must strike out for ourselves in the course of material achievement, and by our own effort and energy present to the world those forces by which the progress of man is judged.

The Negro needs a nation and a country of his own, where he can best show evidence of his own ability in the art of human progress. Scattered as an unmixed and unrecognized part of alien nations and civilizations is but to demonstrate his imbecility, and point him out as an unworthy derelict, fit neither for the society of Greek, Jew nor Gentile.

It is unfortunate that we should so drift apart, as a race, as not to see that we are but perpetuating our own sorrow and disgrace in failing to appreciate the first great requisite of all peoples—organization.

Organization is a great power in directing the affairs of a race or nation toward a given goal. To properly develop the desires that are uppermost, we must first concentrate through some system or method, and there is none better than organization. Hence, the Universal Negro Improvement Association appeals to each and every

Negro to throw in his lot with those of us who, through organization, are working for the universal emancipation of our race and the redemption of our common country, Africa.

No Negro, let him be American, European, West Indian, or African, shall be truly respected until the race as a whole has emancipated itself, through self-achievement and progress, from universal prejudice. The Negro will have to build his own government, industry, art, science, literature, and culture, before the world will stop to consider him. Until then, we are but wards of a superior race and civilization, and the outcasts of a standard social system.

The race needs workers at this time, not plagiarists, copyists, and mere imitators, but men and women who are able to create, to originate and improve, and thus make an independent racial contribution to the world and civilization.

The unfortunate thing about us is that we take the monkey apings of our "so-called leading men" for progress. There is no progress in aping white people and telling us that they represent the best in the race, for in that respect any dressed monkey would represent the best of its species, irrespective of the creative matter of the monkey instinct. The best in a race is not reflected through or by itself. It is such a creation that the Universal Negro Improvement Association seeks.

Let us not try to be the best or worst of others, but let us make the effort to be the best of ourselves. Our own racial critics criticise us as dreamers and "fanatics," and call us "benighted" and "ignorant," because they lack racial backbone. They are unable to see themselves creators of their own needs. The slave instinct has not yet departed from them. They still believe that they can only live or exist through the good graces of their "masters." The good slaves have not yet thrown off their shackles; thus, to them, the Universal Negro Improvement Association is an "impossibility."

It is the slave spirit of dependence that causes our "so-called leading men" (apes) to seek the shelter, leadership, protection, and patronage of the "master" in their organization and so-called advancement work. It is the spirit of feeling secured as good servants of the master, rather than as independents, why our modern Uncle Toms take pride in laboring under alien leadership and becoming surprised at the audacity of the Universal Negro Improvement Association in proclaiming for racial liberty and independence.

But the world of white and other men, deep down in their hearts, have much more respect for those of us who work for our racial salvation under the banner of the Universal Negro Improvement

Association, than they could ever have in all eternity for a group of helpless apes and beggars who make a monopoly of undermining their own race and belittling themselves in the eyes of self-respecting people, by being "good boys" rather than able men.

Surely there can be no good will between apes, seasoned beggars, and independent-minded Negroes who will at least make an effort to do for themselves. Surely, the "dependents" and "wards" (and may I not say racial imbeciles?) will rave against and plan the destruction of movements like the Universal Negro Improvement Association that expose them to the liberal white minds of the world as not being representative of the best in the Negro, but, to the contrary, the worst. The best of a race does not live on the patronage and philanthropy of others, but makes an effort to do for itself. The best of the great white race doesn't fawn before and beg black, brown, or yellow men; they go out, create for self, and thus demonstrate the fitness of the race to survive; and so the white race of America and the world will be informed that the best in the Negro race is not the class of beggars who send out to other races piteous appeals annually for donations to maintain their coterie, but the groups within us that are honestly striving to do for themselves with the voluntary help and appreciation of that class of other races that is reasonable, just, and liberal enough to give to each and every one a fair chance in the promotion of those ideals that tend to greater human progress and human love.

The work of the Universal Negro Improvement Association is clear and clean-cut. It is that of inspiring an unfortunate race with pride in self and with the determination of going ahead in the creation of those ideals that will lift them to the unprejudiced company of races and nations. There is no desire for hate or malice, but every wish to see all mankind linked into a common fraternity of progress and achievement that will wipe away the odor of prejudice, and elevate the human race to the height of real godly love and satisfaction.

PART II

CULTURAL RENAISSANCE
Black Aesthetics and Life-Style

COUNTEE CULLEN

Countee Cullen was New York born and New York centered during most of his life. He was born in 1903 and educated in the city, receiving his undergraduate degree from New York University. He then took graduate work at Harvard University. His first book of poetry, *Color*, was published while he was still a student at NYU. He died in 1946 after a literary career that included a novel and collaboration with Arna Bontemps on a play, *St. Louis Woman*.

Cullen's poem "Heritage" is one of the best known—and most seriously criticized—from the Harlem renaissance. It has been described as exotic and rhapsodic, but it has also been considered a caricature of Africa, much in the same style and mood as Vachel Lindsay's "The Congo." The poem does, however, express the new lyrical mood, if stylistically it is conventional. Cullen is interested in evoking the haunting quality of an African heritage he does not remember and yet wishes to recall.

FURTHER READING: Blanche E. Ferguson. *Countee Cullen and the Negro Renaissance*. New York: Dodd, Mead & Company, 1966.

Countee Cullen

Heritage

What is Africa to me:
Copper sun or scarlet sea.
Jungle star or jungle track,
Strong bronzed men, or regal black
Women from whose loins I sprang
When the birds of Eden sang?
One three centuries removed
From the scenes his fathers loved,
Spicy grove, cinnamon tree,
What is Africa to me?

So I lie, who all day long
Want no sound except the song
Sung by wild barbaric birds
Goading massive jungle herds,
Juggernauts of flesh that pass
Trampling tall defiant grass
Where young forest lovers lie,
Plighting troth beneath the sky.
So I lie, who always hear,
Though I cram against my ear
Both my thumbs, and keep them there,
Great drums throbbing through the air.
So I lie, whose fount of pride,
Dear distress, and joy allied,
Is my somber flesh and skin,
With the dark blood dammed within
Like great pulsing tides of wine

Source: "Heritage" from *On These I Stand* by Countee Cullen. Copyright, 1925, by Harper & Brothers; renewed 1953 by Ida M. Cullen. Reprinted by permission of Harper & Row, Publishers, Inc. Pp. 24-28.

That, I fear, must burst the fine
Channels of the chafing net
Where they surge and foam and fret.

Africa? A book one thumbs
Listlessly, till slumber comes.
Unremembered are her bats
Circling through the night, her cats
Crouching in the river reeds,
Stalking gentle flesh that feeds
By the river brink; no more
Does the bugle-throated roar
Cry that monarch claws have leapt
From the scabbards where they slept.
Silver snakes that once a year
Doff the lovely coats you wear,
Seek no covert in your fear
Lest a mortal eye should see;
What's your nakedness to me?
Here no leprous flowers rear
Fierce corolla in the air;
Here no bodies sleek and wet,
Dripping mingled rain and sweat,
Tread the savage measures of
Jungle boys and girls in love.
What is last year's snow to me,
Last year's anything? The tree
Budding yearly must forget
How its past arose or set—
Bough and blossom, flower, fruit,
Even what shy bird with mute
Wonder at her travail there,
Meekly labored in its hair.
One three centuries removed
From the scenes his fathers loved,
Spicy grove, cinnamon tree,
What is Africa to me?

So I lie, who find no peace
Night or day, no slight release
From the unremittant beat
Made by cruel padded feet
Walking through my body's street.

Up and down they go, and back,
Treading out a jungle track.
So I lie, who never quite
Safely sleep from rain at night—
I can never rest at all
When the rain begins to fall;
Like a soul gone mad with pain
I must match its weird refrain;
Ever must I twist and squirm,
Writhing like a baited worm,
While its primal measures drip
Through my body, crying, "Strip!
Doff this new exuberance.
Come and dance the Lover's Dance!"
In an old remembered way
Rain works on me night and day.

Quaint, outlandish heathen gods
Black men fashion out of rods,
Clay, and brittle bits of stone,
In a likeness like their own,
My conversion came high-priced;
I belong to Jesus Christ,
Preacher of humility;
Heathen gods are naught to me.

Father, Son, and Holy Ghost,
So I make an idle boast;
Jesus of the twice-turned cheek,
Lamb of God, although I speak
With my mouth thus, in my heart
Do I play a double part.
Ever at Thy glowing altar
Must my heart grow sick and falter,
Wishing He I served were black
Thinking then it would not lack
Precedent of pain to guide it,
Let who would or might deride it;
Surely then this flesh would know
Yours had borne a kindred woe.
Lord, I fashion dark gods, too,
Daring even to give You
Dark despairing features where

Crowned with dark rebellious hair,
Patience wavers just so much as
Mortal grief compels, while touches
Quick and hot, of anger, rise
To smitten cheek and weary eyes.
Lord, forgive me if my need
Sometimes shapes a human creed.
All day long and all night through,
One thing only must I do:
Quench my pride and cool my blood,
Lest I perish in the flood.
Lest a hidden ember set
Timber that I thought was wet
Burning like the dryest flax,
Melting like the merest wax,
Lest the grave restore its dead.
Not yet has my heart or head
In the least way realized
They and I are civilized.

LANGSTON HUGHES

Langston Hughes, who enjoys a pre-eminent position among those black artists who formed the Negro renaissance, was born in Joplin, Missouri, in 1902. He attended Columbia University and then left to lead a vagabond's life of exploration, which took him to West Africa, Germany, and France —and which is warmly described in his autobiographical work *The Big Sea*. When he returned to the United States, he had some poetry published and soon was widely recognized (by Vachel Lindsay, among others) as a significant poet. His *The Weary Blues* (1926) is considered one of the most important pieces of literature to emerge from the Negro renaissance, as well as an exciting attempt to translate the mood and rhythm of blues and jazz music into literature. Like Countee Cullen, Hughes looked back upon his African heritage with enthusiasm and expressed his sentiments in two of his best known poems: "The Negro Speaks of Rivers" and "The Negro."

Hughes has maintained a distinguished writing career, which has included the publication of *Not Without Laughter* (1930), *The Ways of White Folks* (1933), *Simple Speaks His Mind* (1950), and a significant anthology of black American poetry.

His article "The Negro Artist and the Racial Mountain" followed an essay by George S. Schuyler, published in *The Nation* earlier and entitled "The Negro-Art Hokum." In his essay Schuyler began with the provocative line, "Negro art 'made in America' is as non-existent as the widely advertised profoundity of Cal Coolidge." Hughes's explanation of the literary condition of the black is an important statement, reverberations of which can be heard today in the opinions of contemporary black writers.

FURTHER READING: James A. Emmanuel. *Langston Hughes*. New York: Twayne Publishers, Inc., 1967.

Langston Hughes

The Negro Artist and the Racial Mountain

One of the most promising of the young Negro poets said to me once, "I want to be a poet—not a Negro poet"; meaning, I believe, "I want to write like a white poet"; meaning subconsciously, "I would like to be a white poet"; meaning behind that, "I would like to be white." And I was sorry the young man said that, for no great poet has ever been afraid of being himself. And I doubted then that, with his desire to run away spiritually from his race, this boy would ever be a great poet. But this is the mountain standing in the way of any true Negro art in America—this urge within the race toward whiteness, the desire to pour racial individuality into the mold of American standardization, and to be as little Negro and as much American as possible.

But let us look at the immediate background of this young poet. His family is of what I suppose one would call the Negro middle class: people who are by no means rich yet never uncomfortable nor hungry—smug, contented, respectable folk, members of the Baptist church. The father goes to work every morning. He is a chief steward at a large white club. The mother sometimes does fancy sewing or supervises parties for the rich families of the town. The children go to a mixed school. In the home they read white papers and magazines. And the mother often says "Don't be like niggers" when the children are bad. A frequent phrase from the father is, "Look how well a white man does things." And so the word "white" comes to be unconsciously a symbol of all the virtues. It holds for the children beauty, morality, and money. The whisper of "I want to be white" runs silently through their minds. This young poet's home is, I believe, a fairly typical home of the colored middle class.

Source: *The Nation*, June 23, 1926, pp. 692–694. Reprinted by permission of Harold Ober Associates, Incorporated. Copyright 1926 by Langston Hughes.

One sees immediately how difficult it would be for an artist born in such a home to interest himself in interpreting the beauty of his own people. He is never taught to see that beauty. He is taught rather not to see it, or if he does, to be ashamed of it when it is not according to Caucasian patterns.

For racial culture the home of a self-styled "high-class" Negro has nothing better to offer. Instead there will perhaps be more aping of things white than in a less cultured or less wealthy home. The father is perhaps a doctor, lawyer, landowner, or politician. The mother may be a social worker, or a teacher, or she may do nothing and have a maid. Father is often dark but he has usually married the lightest woman he could find. The family attend a fashionable church where few really colored faces are to be found. And they themselves draw a color line. In the North they go to white theaters and white movies. And in the South they have at least two cars and a house "like white folks." Nordic manners, Nordic faces, Nordic hair, Nordic art (if any) and an Episcopal heaven. A very high mountain indeed for the would-be racial artist to climb in order to discover himself and his people.

But then there are the low-down folks, the so-called common element, and they are the majority—may the Lord be praised! The people who have their nip of gin on Saturday nights and are not too important to themselves or the community, or too well fed, or too learned to watch the lazy world go round. They live on Seventh Street in Washington or State Street in Chicago and they do not particularly care whether they are like white folks or anybody else. Their joy runs, bang! into ecstasy. Their religion soars to a shout. Work maybe a little today, rest a little tomorrow. Play awhile. Sing awhile. O, let's dance! These common people are not afraid of spirituals, as for a long time their more intellectual brethren were, and jazz is their child. They furnish a wealth of colorful, distinctive material for any artist because they still hold their own individuality in the face of American standardizations. And perhaps these common people will give to the world its truly great Negro artist, the one who is not afraid to be himself. Whereas the better-class Negro would tell the artist what to do, the people at least let him alone when he does appear. And they are not ashamed of him —if they know he exists at all. And they accept what beauty is their own without question.

Certainly there is, for the American Negro artist who can escape the restrictions the more advanced among his own group would put upon him, a great field of unused material ready for his art. Without going outside his race, and even among the better classes with their "white" culture and conscious American manners, but still Negro enough to be different, there is sufficient matter to furnish a black artist with a lifetime of creative work. And when he chooses to touch on the relations between Negroes and whites in this country with their innumerable overtones and undertones, surely, and especially for literature and the drama, there is an inexhaustible supply of themes at hand. To these the Negro artist can give his racial individuality, his heritage of rhythm and warmth, and his incongruous humor that so often, as in the Blues, becomes ironic laughter mixed with tears. But let us look again at the mountain.

A prominent Negro clubwoman in Philadelphia paid eleven dollars to hear Raquel Meller sing Andalusian popular songs. But she told me a few weeks before she would not think of going to hear "that woman," Clara Smith, a great black artist, sing Negro folksongs. And many an upper-class Negro church, even now, would not dream of employing a spiritual in its services. The drab melodies in white folks' hymnbooks are much to be preferred. "We want to worship the Lord correctly and quietly. We don't believe in 'shouting.' Let's be dull like the Nordics," they say, in effect.

The road for the serious black artist, then, who would produce a racial art is most certainly rocky and the mountain is high. Until recently he received almost no encouragement for his work from either white or colored people. The fine novels of Chestnutt go out of print with neither race noticing their passing. The quaint charm and humor of Dunbar's dialect verse brought to him, in his day, largely the same kind of encouragement one would give a sideshow freak (A colored man writing poetry! How odd!) or a clown (How amusing!).

The present vogue in things Negro, although it may do as much harm as good for the budding colored artist, has at least done this: it has brought him forcibly to the attention of his own people among whom for so long, unless the other race had noticed him beforehand, he was a prophet with little honor. I understand that Charles Gilpin acted for years in Negro theaters without any special acclaim from his own, but when Broadway gave him eight curtain calls, Negroes, too, began to beat a tin pan in his honor. I know a young colored writer, a manual worker by day, who had been writing well for the colored magazines for some years, but it was not until he recently broke into the white publications and his first book was accepted by a prominent New York publisher that the "best" Negroes in his city took the trouble to discover that he lived there. Then almost immediately they decided to give a grand dinner for him. But the society ladies were careful to whisper to his mother that perhaps she'd better not come. They were not sure she would have an evening gown.

The Negro artist works against an undertow of sharp criticism and misunderstanding from his own group and unintentional bribes from the whites. "O, be respectable, write about nice people, show how good we are," say the Negroes. "Be stereotyped, don't go too far, don't shatter our illusions about you, don't amuse us too seriously. We will pay you," say the whites. Both would have told Jean Toomer not to write "Cane." The colored people did not praise it. The white people did not buy it. Most of the colored people who did read "Cane" hate it. They are afraid of it. Although the critics gave it good reviews the public remained indifferent. Yet (excepting the work of Du Bois) "Cane" contains the finest prose written by a Negro in America. And like the singing of Robeson, it is truly racial.

But in spite of the Nordicized Negro intelligentsia and the desires of some white editors we have an honest American Negro literature already with us. Now I await the rise of the Negro theater. Our folk music, having achieved world-wide fame, offers itself to the genius of the great individual American Negro composer who is to come. And within the next decade I expect to see the work of a growing school of colored artists who paint and model the beauty of dark faces and create with new technique the expressions of their own soul-world. And the Negro dancers who will dance like flame and the singers who will continue to carry our songs to all who listen—they will be with us in even greater numbers tomorrow.

Most of my own poems are racial in theme and treatment, derived from the life I know. In many of them I try to grasp and hold some of the meanings and rhythms of jazz. I am as sincere as I know how to be in these poems and yet after every reading I answer questions like these from my own people: Do you think Negroes should always write about Negroes? I wish you wouldn't read some of your poems to white folks. How do you find anything interesting in a place like a cabaret? Why do you write about black people? You aren't black. What makes you do so many jazz poems?

But jazz to me is one of the inherent expressions of Negro life in America: the eternal tom-tom beating in the Negro soul—the tom-tom of revolt against weariness in a white world, a world of subway trains, and work, work, work; the tom-tom of joy and laughter, and pain swallowed in a smile. Yet the Philadelphia clubwoman is ashamed to say that her race created it and she does not like me to write about it. The old subconscious "white is best" runs through her mind. Years of study under white teachers, a lifetime of white books, pictures, and papers, and white manners, morals, and Puritan standards made her dislike the spirituals. And now she turns up her nose at jazz and all its manifestations—likewise almost everything else distinctly racial. She doesn't care for the Winold Reiss portraits of Negroes because they are "too Negro." She does not want a true picture of herself from anybody. She wants the artist to flatter her, to make the white world believe that all Negroes are as smug and as near white in soul as she wants to be. But, to my mind, it is the duty of the younger Negro artist, if he accepts any duties at all from outsiders, to change through the force of his art that old whispering "I want to be white," hidden in the aspirations of his people, to "Why should I want to be white? I am a Negro—and beautiful!"

So I am ashamed for the black poet who says, "I want to be a poet—not a Negro poet," as though his own racial world were not as interesting as any other world. I am ashamed, too, for the colored artist who runs from the painting of Negro faces to the painting of sunsets after the manner of the academicians because he fears the strange un-whiteness of his own features. An artist must be free to choose what he does, certainly, but he must also never be afraid to do what he might choose.

Let the blare of Negro jazz bands and the bellowing voice of Bessie Smith singing Blues penetrate the closed ears of the colored near-intellectuals until they listen and perhaps understand. Let Paul Robeson singing "Water Boy" and Rudolph Fisher writing about the streets of Harlem, and Jean Toomer holding the heart of Georgia in his hands, and Aaron Douglas drawing strange black fantasies cause the smug Negro middle class to turn from their white, respectable, ordinary books and papers to catch a glimmer of their own beauty. We younger Negro artists who create now intend to express our individual dark-skinned selves without fear or shame. If white people are pleased we are glad. If they are not, it doesn't matter. We know we are beautiful. And ugly too. The tom-tom cries and the tom-tom laughs. If colored people are pleased we are glad. If they are not, their displeasure doesn't matter either. We build our temples for tomorrow, strong as we know how, and we stand on top of the mountain, free within ourselves.

JEAN PRICE-MARS

Price-Mars was one of the leading figures in the founding of the Haitian renaissance and something of a spiritual father to negritude. Born in Haiti in 1876, he studied medicine both in Paris and in Haiti, but soon entered a diplomatic career that was as long as it was impressive. He served his country as ambassador to the Republic of San Domingo, to the United Nations, and to France. He founded the Haitian Institute of Ethnology and was elected first president of the African Society of Culture, the permanent organization that emerged from the first International Congress of Negro Writers and Artists. In addition to this activity, he was a prodigious author, remaining alert until his death in 1969.

His most famous work was *Ainsi parla l'oncle (So Uncle Said)*, published in 1929. Influential in inspiring Haitians to a realization of the meaning and value of their African past and their folk tradition, this volume is a serious ethnographic investigation. While respecting French culture, Price-Mars argues that the African past, which was so formative in Haitian life, should be glorified and appreciated. Beginning with a discussion of the role played by the fictitious Oncle Bouqui and Ti Malice, he proceeds to a very detailed discussion of Voodoo, tracing its origins back to Dahomey. He also discusses other Africanisms and stresses the role of music and dance in the life of the black man, arguing that "with the Negro their power over the organism takes on a definite biological character."

FURTHER READING: "Hommage à Jean Price-Mars," *Présence africaine*, No. 71, 1969, pp. 3–23.

Jean Price-Mars

From *Ainsi parla l'oncle*

The Haitian people have manifested a scarcely disguised discomfort, even something bordering on abhorrence, whenever their distant past is spoken of; a disconcerting paradox for they have one of the most engaging and moving, if not one of the most beautiful histories of the world—that of the transplantation of a human race to alien soil in the severest of biological conditions. This condition has resulted from the fact that those people, who because—armed with force and science—were able to be the artisans of black servitude for over four hundred years, have distorted the Haitian historical adventure by stating that Negroes were the outcasts of humanity, without a history, without morality, without religion, and had to be infused by whatever means available with new moral values, outfitted with a new humanity. When, as a result of the crises of change precipitated by the French Revolution, the community of slaves in San Domingo rose up and demanded rights which no one had previously dreamed of granting them, the success of their claims proved to be both a difficulty and a surprise to them: the difficulty of choosing a social discipline, the surprise at the adaptation of a heterogeneous herd of people to the stable life of free labor. Obviously the simplest way out for the revolutionaries, in a state of national disunity, was to copy the only model offered to their minds. Thus, for better and for worse, they inserted the new social grouping into the dislocated framework of a scattered white society. It was in this manner that the Negro community of Haiti donned the cast-off attire of Western Civilization after 1804. From then on, with a persistency that no setback, sarcasm, or upheaval could hope to deflect, the Haitian community strove to realize what it believed to be its higher destiny by modelling its thoughts and sentiments on an approximation of

---

Source: Jean Price-Mars, *Ainsi parla l'oncle* (Paris: Compiègne, 1929), pp. i–iv, 219–222, 232–233, 235–236. Selections translated by the editor.

France, by attempting to resemble that country and by identifying with it. An absurd and grandiose task! A difficult task if ever there was one!

But this is an example of that curious occurrence which, in the metaphysics of M. Gaultier, is called a collective bovaryism, that is, the quality by which a society is able to conceive of itself in terms other than it is. A strikingly rich attitude, if the society in question has the means for a creative activity which would lead to an improvement over its present condition. In this event, the quality of imagining itself other than it is becomes an incentive, a powerful force which drives it on to overcome the obstacles found in its forward-directing and ascending path. However, such is a singularly dangerous attitude if the society is weighted down with impedimentia, stuck in the ruts of routine and servile imitation, because then the society seems to make no contribution to the complex play of human progress and will, sooner or later, provide the surest pretext for being wiped off the map by those nations impatient for territorial expansion and ambitious to establish their hegemony. Despite some effort toward alteration and some occasional perception of the situation, it was by the application of the second point of the previously described dilemma that Haiti found its place among the world's peoples. There was, of course, the possibility that the effort would be considered without interest and originality. But, by an irresistible logic, the more we forced ourselves to believe that we were "colored" Frenchmen, the more we simply forgot to be Haitian, which is to say, men born in historically determined conditions, having acquired in our souls, as have all human groups, a psychological complex which gave to the Haitian community its specific form. At that point, everything which was authentically indigenous —language, mores, sentiments, beliefs—became suspect, tarnished with bad taste in the eyes of the elites seized with nostalgia for the lost mother country. As this process occurred, the word "negro," formerly a generic term, acquired a pejorative meaning. As for that of "African," it always has been and is the most humiliating term by which a Haitian can be addressed. Strictly speaking, the most distinguished person in this country would rather that someone found a resemblance between him and an Eskimo or a Samoan or a Tongan rather than to recall his Guinean or Sudanese origins. One should see with what pride several of our most representative personalities suggest the actual existence of some bastard line of descent. All the baseness of colonial promiscuities, the anonymous disgraces of accidental encounters, the brief coupling of two paroxysms, have become the titles of consideration and of glory. What can be the future, what can be the value of a society where such aberrations of judgment, such mistakes of orientation are formed into basic opinions. A very difficult problem for those who are reflective and who have the task of meditating on the social conditions of our environment!

* * *

But, one might say, what is the purpose of so much bother over such minute problems which interest but a very small minority of men living on a very small part of the terrestrial surface?

Perhaps this question is sound.

However, we will allow ourselves the objection that neither the smallness of our territory nor the numerical weakness of our people is sufficient reason for the dismissal by the rest of humanity of those problems which affect the behavior of a group of people. Moreover, our presence on a point of this American archipelago that we have "humanized," the breach we have made in the historical process in order to grasp our place among men, our method of employing the laws of imitation in order to give us an imitative spirit, the pathological deviation that we have imposed on group bovaryism by conceiving ourselves as other than we are, the tragic uncertainty that such a step marks on our evolution at the time when all sorts of imperialisms are disguising their exploitations with the veil of philanthropy—all of that gives a certain relief to the existence of the Haitian community and, before night falls, it is not without purpose to collect the facts of our social life, to determine the deeds and the attitudes of our people, no matter how humble they may be, and to compare them with those of other peoples, to scrutinize their origins, and to situate them in the general existence of man on this planet. These are all factors whose significance cannot be negligible in any judgment of the worth of one part of the human race.

* * *

But, in fact, what is the origin of the greater part of the customs that we have spoken about? Are they derived from the local scene or did they really come to us from overseas?

About this matter one can well conjecture. None of them is altogether a local creation, but also none has come to us without alteration. They are like our personality itself, all charged with reminiscences and impressed by the successive mutations which mark the complexity of our ethnic origins. Since our evolution as a people occurred in divergent directions, such that a small number among us has acquired an intellectual and social culture which makes it a world apart—very proud and vain in its ivory tower and having only a distant and formal contact with the rest of the population lost in misery and ignorance—it is among the multitude that we will have the best chance of again finding the thread of oral traditions derived from overseas. When one submits these traditions to a comparative examination, they immediately reveal that Africa, for the most part is their land of origin.

But just as the beliefs from which they derive . . . divide Africa into distinct zones, so the map of related mores and customs covers the greater part of the Western portion of the Old Continent.

Would you like to be present, comparatively speaking, at the founding of a family in some part of the Congo, the Sudan, or Dahomey?

Ah! I know what repugnance I will encounter in daring to speak to you of Africa and African matters! The subject seems unelegant and completely devoid of interest to you, doesn't it?

Be careful, my friends, that such attitudes do not derive from scandalous ignorance. We live on ideas gone stale by the prodigious absurdity of a poorly arranged culture, and our childish vanity is only satisfied when we recite phrases written by others or when we glorify the notion that "the Gauls were our ancestors."

Well, we only will have the opportunity of being ourselves if we do not repudiate any part of our ancestral heritage. Now, this heritage is eight-tenths a gift of Africa. Moreover, on this small planet which is only an infinitesimal point in space, men have been so mixed for thousands of years that no true intellectual, not even in the United States of America, could uphold the theory of pure races without laughing. If I understand the real science of Sir Harry Johnston, there is not a single Negro whatsoever in the heart of Africa who does not have some drops of Caucasoid blood in his veins and perhaps not a single white man, even the proudest in the United Kingdom, in France, in Spain, or elsewhere, who does not have some drops of Negro or yellow blood in his veins. Such is the truth found in the verse of the poet: "All men are man."

Our ancestors? But why should I be embarrassed to know from whence they came, if I carry my sign of human dignity on my forehead like a radiant star and if in my upward movement toward more understanding, I am lightened by the sacred wound of the ideal?

Our ancestors? They are first the dead whose earthly sufferings, courage, intelligence, and sensitivity were blended in the crucible of San Domingo in order to make us what we are: free men. Our ancestors? They are the dead, with combined virtues and vices, who speak softly in our wretched hearts or to our heroic and noble conscience.

Our ancestors? they are those who slowly lifted themselves from primitive animalism to lead toward the transitory beings that we now are, still trembling before the unknown which surrounds us, but heirs to the unfading glory of being men. It is because our ancestors were men who suffered, who loved and who hoped, that we, we also can aspire to the full dignity of being men despite the brutal insolence of all kinds of imperialism.

Whites, blacks, mulattos, *griffes,* octoroons, quatroons, marabouts, *sacatras:* of what significance are these labels from the rejected colonial situation if we believe ourselves to be men resolved to play fully our role as men on this small part of the global scene which is our Haitian society.

Therefore, accept the ancestral patrimony as a block. Walk around it, weigh it, examine it with intelligence and circumspection, and you will see, as if in a broken mirror, that it reflects a reduced image of all of mankind. Yes, the same causes have produced the same effects on the entire surface of the planet. Love, hunger, fear have engendered the same tales in the passionate imagination of men, whether they lived in the all-encircling bush of the Sudan, whether they formerly appeared on the hills where the Acropolis arose or on the banks of the Tiber where the city of the Seven Hills was erected. And this is why the African today provides the sociologist with the elements from which he is able to establish the psychology of primitive man. The constitution of the family is above all for him an act of faith, a religious ceremony of initiation. Such it was in ancient Greece and Rome, and so it is in certain tribes in the Sudan, Dahomey, the Congo—except for the inevitable variations created by the circumstance and necessities of the physical surroundings.

* * *

By way of conclusion it remains for us to draw some lessons from the ethnographic comparisons we have made. First, there exists in the marriage ceremony some striking analogies between the customs of classical Greece and Rome and those which are still observed in certain parts of Africa. In addition, our peasant populations on this side of the Atlantic are imbued with these customs also. On all sides one observes the same symbolism which makes the union of man and wife an eminently religious act. One finds almost the same ritual and propitiary sacrifice which obligates the young couple to the gods of the family, the village, and the tribe; nearly the same symbolism which leads to the choice of the white veil and crown, the white loin cloth, powder and clay as exterior signs of the new life. Just as today in our world the white veil, the orange flower crown and the white robe are emblems of purity and innocence of the virgin who desires to begin the marital life. Dare I say, gentlemen, that your white ties and gloves are perhaps also outer signs of your purity, of intentions that you bring to the hearth?

In all cases, in Greece, in Rome, and in Africa, man is the master consecrated by ancient custom.

Head of the family, having the responsibility to group around him the gods and ancestors, it is he alone who can authorize who will be allowed to approach the altar where the sacrifice to the titular divinity is made. Whether this thought be more formalized there than here, none of it is absent even if it exists only in a state of survival. It seems to me that a very important social fact derives from these various remarks: if the marriage ceremony is cloaked in such a quality of religious solemnity here as there, it likewise implies the idea of the gravity attached to it, and it implies that the constitution of the family is in close alliance with the continuity of the religious cult and the well-being of the village or the tribe. From this mysterious quality derives the solidity of family ties. Certainly this is true in certain of the regions of Africa about which we have spoken, where a small community is protected by the eldest male who is the natural chief; he is the elder. The union of these communities in a given space forms the village, ruled by a chief chosen among the elders and whose wisdom and experience are appreciated. Can you imagine in these conditions the power of family ties formed in such a conjuncture? Such a condition has constantly been pointed out by Africologists. They state how much the young Negro is attached to his village, to his family group, and particularly to that person who is the living incarnation of it: his mother.

* * *

Do you know why the godmother in San Domingo has nearly replaced the mother in the child's affection? It is because most often the hardly-weaned child is snatched from this mother whose services are needed for economic exploitation. He henceforth hardly knows anyone but his godmother, while he too awaits the moment when he will become another number in the labor workshop. The deep reason for such a cruel disorder is found in the destructive action exercised by slavery on the social economy of the black, such that this monstrous system has been perpetuated for four centuries by the white race on the black race. Ah, my friends, my heart is not large enough to contain all the love I feel for mankind. I therefore have no room for hatred. But I cannot check myself from the horror of the thought of the carnage and destruction pursued here and on the old continent with an implacable method by those who pride themselves on being a superior humanity, and who now dare reproach the black race for its savagery and institutional instability.

Yes, for four hundred years, the white race, without pity or mercy, aroused internecine war in Africa, pitting Negro against Negro, chasing them without respite or mercy, in order to satisfy this ignoble traffic in human flesh and, in so doing, destroying all native civilization and culture. Then, for another two centuries, the white sailed his boats loaded with human cattle to the shores of this island already bloody from the extermination of the Indian; and during these two centuries of outrageous promiscuity, corruption, and degeneracy, the white soiled the ancient chastity of the Negress and imposed on her the brutal law of concubinage. It is thus that the organization of Negro life was ripped, destroyed, and annihilated by the saddest abomination which has ever stained the face of the earth. The truth of this fact is shown following upon 1804. Then our fathers, in adopting without the slightest concern a legal and religious statute which was so different from their old social concepts, surrendered themselves without thinking about it to the most formidable experience which men have ever endeavored.

For over a hundred years what has been the result? You can see it in this confusion of mores, beliefs, and customs from which slowly emerged a new social order. Perhaps it is now only a chrysalid which causes indignation, mockery, or embarrassment for the impatient, the myopic, and the ignorant, but which philosophers and men of spirit watch attentively and with interest. What will it become in one, two, or five hundred years? I certainly do not know. But what were those nations and people who today have become rotten from pompous display, prejudices, and hatred when for over nineteen centuries a magnificent civilization flourished on the banks of the Nile? What were they? Miserable barbarians, history answers.

Men pass by; it is perhaps good that they are not eternal.

This is why those among us who make a profession of investigating the historical and ethnic origins of Haitian people are captivated by the dazzling intuition that its past will reply to its future. But, for heaven's sake, my friends, do not scorn our ancestral patrimony. Love it, consider it as an intangible whole. Rather, repeat the proud statement that the ancient bard placed in the mouth of an inhabitant of Mount Olympus: "There is nothing ugly in my father's house."

LOUIS-THOMAS ACHILLE

Louis-Thomas Achille, born in Martinique in 1909, is a cousin of Paulette Nardal, one of the founders of the *Revue du monde noir*. Achille had been recommended by Alain Locke for a teaching position in French at Howard University, a position he accepted and held for some ten years between 1932 and 1943. Achille provided "one important link between black Americans in Paris and the *Revue du monde noir*," according to Professor Mercer Cook of Howard University. Achille now makes his home in France, where he has been professor at the Lycée du Parc in Lyon and also has been a contributor to *Présence africaine, Esprit,* and *Crisis*.

The two essays reproduced here appeared in the *Revue du monde noir* under the title "Art and the Blacks." They are by far the most significant of the articles published in that periodical and clearly indicate a mood and theme that most closely resembles negritude. Although Achille did not employ the term, his assessment of what he believes to be the black's artistic instinct is a prologue to what Léopold Sédar Senghor would later comment on. It is true that Price-Mars had already touched upon the theme of the rhythmic nature of the black, but it is Achille who provides one of the first, if not the first assertive and meaningful explanation of the role of music and dance in the spiritual-psychological makeup of the black peoples.

Louis-Thomas Achille
Art and the Blacks

Blacks are fundamentally artists. This is a quality which has universally been recognized as theirs since the diffusion of both Negro-American music and dances and of African sculpture. In truth there is no other human race in which the aesthetic sense is so widely distributed and so constantly intervenes in the activity of each individual. What is the characteristic of a few isolated individuals in other races is the characteristic of the entire black race, both in its ethnically pure elements and in those where racial intermixture has not blunted the sharpest racial characteristics. Among blacks one discovers less an aesthetic *taste*, the exercise of which requires a necessary and primary participation of the intelligence (representation of designs, colors, sculptural or literary forms, canons, rules concerning genres, etc.) than an artistic *instinct* requiring urgent and frequent satisfaction for the *body* as well as for the mind. Deeply penetrating the entire organism, even down to the minutest nerve fibers and tissues most removed from the vital centers of the heart and brain, this instinct stimulates and imposes actual physical needs. Art, therefore, is no longer a leisure-time activity, an incidental matter that can easily be done without, given one's preoccupation with more basic needs. It is an activity of fundamental importance like drinking and eating—and nearly as sensual as these. Art does not place the individual in an exceptional and somewhat abnormal situation. On the contrary, it constitutes for him a truly natural function, among the most normal, and for which this vast organ, which is the human body, has been constructed.

Such an aesthetic constitution predisposes the black race more to artistic sensation than to artistic production, but without condemning it to sterile activity. Far from that. Must the race itself not produce

---

Source: *Revue du monde noir*, No. 1 (November 1931), pp. 53–56, and No. 2 (December 1931), pp. 28–31. Selections translated by the editor; reprinted by permission of the author.

and utilize the artistic nourishment appropriate to its own particular shape, that which is most likely to satisfy its need for art? Yet, having to choose from among the diverse art forms, it will most readily turn to that form which, when produced, will be immediately accompanied by an intense artistic sensation. This is the reason why blacks, whether from Africa or America, are above all dancers. Above all, because the dance is the most immediately realized work of art. Immediately, in time: no need as in sculpture or in painting for tools or materials which are often difficult to obtain quickly, and which generally require long and laborious usage. On the contrary, the dance requires nothing but a command from the brain, or, even less yet, a muscular reflex to a musical stimulus, perhaps simply to a tonal stimulus (providing it is rhythmic); and then and there is created one of the movements the sequence of which will be a work of art. Immediately, also in space: no tool is interposed between the artist creating and the object created. One and the other fuse. The artist is the art object. His vegetative life flows over into the plastic or rhythmic forms of the art object. Man becomes Beauty, even to the stamping of the soles of the feet and the gyration of the hips. The work of art itself is the source of the aesthetic rapture it arouses, a true artistic delirium resulting from a double joy: the feeling that one is creating and is also the thing created. The imagination can hardly grasp the fact that an entire race can possess such an intense faculty for aesthetic creation and emotion, in much the same way that other races have, for example, the rich faculty for wondering. However, this aesthetic faculty resides somber and silent under the skin of color and is activated into attitudes or movements which are rich in Beauty from the very moment a series of its rhythms is heard.

In these conditions it should not be surprising to learn that the blacks, for a long time isolated in Africa from all outside influence, or not having found in Europe or America a form suitable to their sensibility, have until now produced very little in painting. But the evolution of "white" painting and engraving towards a form of expression more immediate, closer to brute sensation; and the progressive adaptation of black sensibility to a mode of artistic expression never instinctively sought are giving birth to a black pictorial art of which the first French and American examples are most promising. I will speak more fully of this later.

Sculpture, on the contrary, was often and over a long period of time, practiced by the blacks of Africa. It is this activity which brought them their first and most distinguished admirers in Europe.

However, the number of works in this art form is not at all proportionate to the extent and depth of the artistic expression of the race. This curious disproportion is explained by geographical, historical, religious, and social circumstances. It is surprising to note in a race so profoundly artistic that it is not generally from pure and disinterested artistic inspiration that the blacks have sculpted in wood those admirable ritual masks or commemorative masks which we have the pleasure to contemplate in public and private collections and at the Parisian Colonial Exposition. Religious purpose in fact guided the hand of the artisan, and, as he was also an artist, the result was a beautiful work of art. Although a similar development has not always been the case with all branches of the black race, the genius of the artist has exhibited the same profound racial qualities, even where it has freely developed. This particular point has been commented on in recent studies dedicated to African sculpture and other art forms. In a race so inherently artistic, all branches of human activity are permeated by artistic considerations. The aesthetic emotion, always present, fills the individual with a source of constant happiness which often spares him from exhaustingly searching for other satisfactions. Here is doubtlessly the origin of the "loud laughter of the Negro" which continues from birth to death, and from Africa to America. Might not one find in all of this a partial explanation for the long and mysterious stagnation of African society, a society exempted from intensive activity in the political, economic, and intellectual order by the generous and constant consumption of human activity in incessant artistic manifestations?

In the previous essay, which it would be pretentious to call the aesthetic psychophysiology of the black, I attempted to explain the particular reaction of the black to Beauty. I will now inquire into those modes of artistic expression toward which the blacks of the entire world tend to gravitate, despite the diversity of the civilizations in which they now live and the different regions of the world where they have been disseminated throughout history.

The study of the aesthetic nature of the black allows one to affirm a priori that wherever racial mixture has only modified superficial ethnic characteristics such as the color of the skin, for example, the dance will be the preferred mode of artistic creation for the black. Facts are easily found to corroborate this deduction. No race dances as much as the Negro race. Among blacks, everything ends not with a song but with a ball. Colored people can hardly imagine a general get-together which will not be a "dancing." America, then Europe and Paris in particular have witnessed the blacks assuming an increasingly significant place in the world which dances: Negro balls are multiplying. Of course it is true that one will hardly find here the original atmosphere of the Antillean "casinos" or the Negro dancehalls in Harlem, but their number speaks for itself. Colonials and African explorers are commonly surprised by the frequency and the enthusiasm of the dances, which, nevertheless, seem to leave the dancers unsatiated.

The nature of African, Antillean, or American choreographic development proves once more the common ancestry of these diverse black groupings, if it should by chance be disputed. Without doubt an inattentive observer would not immediately discover a great similarity among certain, rapid, abrupt, and vigorous African dances; the languorous and undulating movements of the Antillean beguine; and the raucous Charleston and the extravagant cakewalk. But beneath these differences, easily explained by environmental diversity, many common qualities can be found: for example, the particular importance of rhythm, the search for difficult syncopation, the expression of delight or seriousness, of sincere conviction revealed on the faces of the dancers, etc. Antilleans and Americans retain from their far-off "African past" an atavistic attachment to certain rhythms of the Dark Continent of which they intellectually ignore even the existence: but at the first sound of the tom-toms they react with an instinctive mechanism. That which the mind and the heart might have been able to unlearn, the muscles and the nerves still recall. By the same token, Africans clearly acknowledge the Negro inspiration in certain "pretty tunes" ["bels-airs"] or "lagghias" from the Antilles. Thus, a certain relative and easily recognizable psychological identity is maintained under the diversity of customs, mentalities, and outlook.

After the dance comes music, but at a much lower level, because of the subservient position in which the choreographic art places it. Until about fifty years ago, it could have been said that music in a Negro country hardly existed except to accompany the dance. The latter even imposed upon it certain laws, essentially rhythmic, thus creating for the ear the same need for a rhythm as that heretofore localized in the limbs—to use a simplistic physiology. Even separated from the dance, music still submits to that law. How many African melodies, purely lyrical songs, irresistibly evoke the pounding of the tom-toms and the movements of the dancers! For many young Antilleans, provided with an ordinary secondary school education and not at all unaware of classical music, "to make music" signifies to enjoy the dance airs. Finally, the American "spirituals," hymns, and canticles of religious devotion, differ so little in rhythm from dance airs, that the faithful, singing in the church, are unconsciously led to suggest "swings" and "jerks." It is in the form of European civilization, imported into America, that Antilleans and Americans must, among other things, recognize the possibilities of a musical genius full of delicacy and vitality. The contemporary compositions of Harry T. Burleigh and R. Nathaniel Dett in the United States, and of Mme. Maiotte Almaby in Martinique are remarkable proofs of this.

If sculpture in the Antilles and the United States did not witness the creation of any work dignified enough to be singled out (with the exception of the last half-century), it inspired too many African artists for it not to be considered one of the favorite art forms of blacks. This might appear to be a surprising phenomenon, for sculpture must have proven to be a formidable competitor to gain favor with a race of dancers. Dance and sculpture seem indeed to be as opposed as movement and stability, heat and cold, life and death. These two art forms, however, are intensively cultivated by the same race, often by the same individuals. And for the reason that they both satisfy tendencies which are often the same: love of the form and lines exposed by a nude dancer and by a fetish statue; love of the intense vitality which is exhibited in choreographic activities and in the expression of tension in certain sculpted figures, in their posture constantly suggesting the possibility of instantaneous movements.

Sculpture, moreover, satisfies Negro sensualism by providing the senses with a suggestive reproduction of familiar objects. In this regard it is better than painting which is a cheating and lying form of art, pretending to suggest nature to us while suppressing the dimensions of space. Children, hardly habituated to abstraction, are not content with the sketch of a doll, while a molded or sculpted doll gives them pleasure. And so it is with primitive peoples who, in looking at a statue, would like to believe in some vague way that it is the resurrection of the known living being. It is worth noting that this belief generally finds no basis in the realism of the reproduction, for nearly all Negro sculptors tend to stylize their subjects. The belief rests in the fact that the work of art is visible, tangible, sonorous, weighty, upright, in the manner of the being, man or beast, that it is supposed to represent. Religion supports this sensualism with an animism which endows each statue with a personal, physical, and moral life, thus achieving the assimilation between the work of art and nature.

The preceding factors are several of the reasons which make of sculpture one of the favorite arts of blacks and are factors which also constitute the characteristics of this "primitive" sculpture. Will one find these latter characteristics among contemporary black artists trained in the European or Europeanized American school of art? This much is certain: modern white culture tends to make these characteristics disappear. But, as a result, does not the artist endure a regrettable loss? It certainly would be interesting to know the experiences of contemporary Negro sculptors on this subject. The very question can, moreover, be asked of all artists, better yet, of all men of color who have assimilated European culture. It might even take an amusing turn, if one were to use the traditional opposition dear to simplistic souls: What still remains in you of the savage, and what is there of the civilized person?

AIMÉ CÉSAIRE

Aimé Césaire was born in Fort de France, Martinique, in 1913. After his secondary education there, he left for Paris in 1931 and studied at the Lycée Louis le Grand and then the École normale supérieure. His friendship with Léopold Senghor dates from the time they jointly founded, with the poet Léon Damas, the publication *Étudiant noir*. Senghor has been lavish in his praise of Césaire and in his recognition of Césaire's contribution to the poetry of negritude. Upon completion of his studies, Césaire returned to Martinique where he became professor at the Lycée Schoelcher and later mayor of Fort de France. Presently a member of the French National Assembly, he enjoys the reputation of a well-respected man of letters.

Césaire was "discovered" by the Surrealist poet André Breton, who read the *Cahier* while in Martinique in 1940. Finding its quality unusual and its style most appealing, Breton announced the work's worth to the French public in an introduction he provided the 1947 edition. The *Cahier*, having been written prior to Césaire's return to Martinique, had first gone unnoticed when it appeared in 1939.

Most critics recognize the surrealistic influences on the poem; some have compared it to the work of the nineteenth-century French poets Mallarmé and Rimbaud; one critic has been nearly tempted to describe it as a "lyrical autobiography." What all agree on is the power of the language, the rich images it evokes, the Caribbean world it discovers, the tenacity with which it clings to the native land wracked by colonialism. Césaire's "return" was the French introduction to poetic negritude.

FURTHER READING: Judith Gleason. "An Introduction to the Poetry of Aimé Césaire," *Negro Digest*, January 1970, pp. 12–19, 64–65.

Aimé Césaire

From *Cahier d'un retour
au pays natal*

O friendly light
O fresh source of light
those who have invented neither gunpowder nor compass
those who tamed neither steam nor electricity
those who explored neither the sea nor the sky
but those without whom the earth would not be the earth
gibbosity all the more beneficent, as the deserted earth is
   all the more earth
silo where is ripened and preserved what is earthiest in earth
my Negritude is not a stone, its deafness thrown against
   the clamour of the day
my Negritude is not a speck of dead water on the dead eye of earth
my Negritude is neither a tower nor a cathedral

it thrusts into the red flesh of the soil
it thrusts into the warm flesh of the sky
it digs under the opaque dejection of its rightful patience

Eia for the royal *Kailcedrat!*
Eia for those who invented nothing
for those who have never discovered
for those who have never conquered

but, struck, deliver themselves to the essence of all things,
ignorant of surfaces, but taken by the very movement of things
not caring to conquer, but playing the game of the world

truly the elder sons of the world
porous to all the breath of the world

Source: *Return to My Native Land* by Aimé Césaire, published by *Présence africaine*, Paris (1968), pp. 99–109, 123–125. Reprinted by permission of the publisher.

fraternal space of all the breath of the world
bed without drain of all the waters in the world
spark of the sacred fire of the world
flesh of the flesh of the world
panting with the very movement of the world
Tepid dawn of ancestral virtues

Blood! Blood! All our blood stirred by the male heart of the sun
Those who know the feminine nature of the moon's oily flesh
the reconciled exultation of the antelope and the star
those whose survival moves in the germination of grass *Eia!*
perfect circle of the world and close concordance!

Hear the white world
horribly fatigued by its immense effort
its rebellious articulations crack under the hard stars
its inflexibilities of blue steel pierce the mystic flesh
hear its treacherous victories trumpeting its defeats
hear with grandiose alibis the pitiful stumbling
Mercy for our omniscient and naive conquerors!

Eia for grief at the udders of reincarnated tears
For those who explored nothing
For those who never mastered

Eia for joy
Eia for love
Eia for grief at the udders of reincarnated tears

Here at the end of the dawn is my virile prayer
that I may not hear the laughter or the cries,
my eyes fixed on this city which I prophesy shall be beautiful
give me the savage faith of the sorcerer
give my hands the power to mould
give my soul the sword's temper
I won't evade. Make my head a prow

and of myself, my heart, make neither a father nor a brother
nor a son, but the father, the brother, the son,
not the husband, but the lover of this unique people.

Make me refractory to vanity, but docile to their genius
as the fist to the extended arm!

make me commissar of their blood
make me trustee of their resentments

make me a man of termination
make me a man of initiation
make me a man of meditation
but also make me a man of germination

make me the executioner of these mighty deeds
this is the time to gird one's loins like a valiant man

but so doing, my heart, preserve me from all hatred
do not make me that man of hate for whom
I feel nothing but hate
for cantonned in this unique race
you know, however, that my tyrannical love
is not out of hatred for other races
that I am the toiler of this unique race
what I want
is for the universal hunger
for the universal thirst

I call the race to be finally free
to produce out of its closed intimacy
the succulence of fruit.

*   *   *

And we are standing now, my country and I, hair in the wind,
my little hand now in its enormous fist, and force is not in us,
but above us, in a voice which pierces the night and the audience
like the sting of an apocalyptic hornet.
And the voice declares that for centuries Europe has stuffed us
with lies and bloated us with pestilence.
for it is not true that the work of man is finished

that we have nothing to do in the world
that we are parasites in the world
that we have only to accept the way of the world

but the work of man has only begun

and it remains for man to conquer all prohibitions immobilized
in the corners of his fervour
and no race has a monopoly of beauty, intelligence, strength
and there is room for all at the rendez-vous of conquest and we know
that the sun turns around our earth, lighting only the portion that our
single will has fixed and that every star falls from sky to earth at
our limitless command.

LÉOPOLD SÉDAR SENGHOR

Léopold Sédar Senghor is Africa's most well-known intellectual and one of her outstanding political leaders. Born in Joal in Senegal in 1903, he was educated in Dakar, then proceeded to Paris where, like Aimé Césaire, he attended the Lycée Louis le Grand and thereafter the Sorbonne. He was the first African student to pass the *agrégation,* a highly competitive examination by which French lycée and university teachers are selected. From 1935 to 1940 he taught in a French lycée. After the Second World War he entered politics and became Senegal's deputy to the French National Assembly; he quickly rose to the pre-eminent position in Senegalese politics. When Senegal became independent, Senghor was elected her president, a position he has held ever since.

As the outstanding advocate of negritude and as a poet of front-rank quality, Senghor has received considerable critical attention. His first book of poetry, *Chants d'ombre,* reflects his early years in Paris when he felt uprooted and when he looked longingly back to his Senegalese childhood. "Femme noire" ("Black Woman") is the most famous of the poems in this collection and is a celebration of idealized African beauty. The publication of *Hosties noires* in 1948 has been widely considered as emblematic of the change of Senghor's mood: from personal to political, from nostalgic to nationalist poetry.

The emerging philosophy of negritude derived from several sources, through Senghor's reading of Teilhard de Chardin, Karl Marx, and Jean-Paul Sartre. If negritude was the "sum total of the African's cultural values," it was not conceived of as a philosophy in belligerent competition with others. Senghor's major concern was with the universal and the harmony of humanity; he believed that African civilization should enrich world culture and could thereby make a major contribution to mankind.

The following essay, entitled in French "L'esprit de la civilisation ou les lois de la culture négro-africaine," was presented at the First International Congress of Black Writers and Artists, held at the Sorbonne between September 19 and September 22, 1956. Probably Senghor's most perceptive and influential assessment of the spirit and meaning of negritude, the essay also remains one of the major statements of black culture made by anyone.

Since the writing of this essay, Senghor has provided further elucidations and modifications of negritude and has moved on to philosophical concern with African socialism and *Africainété*.

FURTHER READING: Irving Markowitz. *Léopold Sédar Senghor and the Politics of Negritude.* New York: Atheneum. 1969.

Léopold Sédar Senghor

Black Woman

Naked woman, black woman
Clothed with your colour which is life, with your form which
 is beauty!
In your shadow I have grown up; the gentleness of your hands
 was laid over my eyes
And now, high up on the sun-baked pass, at the heart of summer,
 at the heart of noon, I come upon you, my Promised Land,
And your beauty strikes me to the heart like the flash of an eagle.

Naked woman, dark woman
Firm-fleshed ripe fruit, sombre raptures of black wine,
 mouth making lyrical my mouth
Savannah stretching to clear horizons, savannah shuddering
 beneath the East Wind's eager caresses
Carved tom-tom, taut tom-tom, muttering under
 the Conqueror's fingers
Your solemn contralto voice is the spiritual song of the Beloved.

Naked woman, dark woman
Oil that no breath ruffles, calm oil on the athlete's flanks,
 on the flanks of the Princes of Mali
Gazelle limbed in Paradise, pearls are stars on the night of your skin
Delights of the mind, the glinting of red gold against
 your watered skin
Under the shadow of your hair, my care is lightened
by the neighbouring suns of your eyes.

Source: From *Prose and Poetry* by Léopold Sédar Senghor, translated by John Reed and Clive Wake, published by Oxford University Press in Three Crowns Books, by permission; also from *Selected Poems* by Léopold Sédar Senghor. Translated by John Reed and Clive Wake. Copyright © Oxford University Press 1964. Reprinted by permission of Atheneum Publishers.

Naked woman, black woman,
I sing your beauty that passes, the form that I fix in the Eternal,
Before jealous Fate turn you to ashes to feed the roots of life.

African-Negro Aesthetics

The twentieth century will be known as the period of the discovery of African-Negro civilization. At first it was the sculpture alone that provoked amazement, shock, and finally admiration. But soon Europe discovered stories, poetry, music, painting, and philosophy, in turn.

Now that the first surprise has had its effect, we must define the spirit of the civilization; that is to say, of African-Negro culture. There is nothing more revealing in this regard than the literature and the art of this singularly "machineless civilization." Philosophical reflection on art, by which aesthetics is defined, is all the more necessary, since the admiration of certain European intellectuals for African-Negro literature and art is not devoid of confusion; it often consists of misconceptions, if not of contradictions in terms.

But before attempting to clarify the fundamental laws of African-Negro art I must speak of the black man who has worked out an original culture, and I must first outline his physiopsychology.

It has often been said that the Negro is a man of nature. He lives traditionally off the land and with the land, in accordance with the cosmos. He is a sensualist, a being whose senses are exposed. He is without intermediary between subject and object; these are, for him, simultaneous. He is first of all sounds, odors, rhythms, forms, and colors; I mean that he is touch before he is sight, unlike the white European. He feels more than he sees; he feels himself. It is within himself, within his flesh, that he receives and senses the radiations that any existing object emits. Aroused, he responds to the appeal and lets himself go, moving from subject to object, from me to thou, on the waves of the Other. He dies within himself to be reborn in the Other. He is not assimilated; he assimilates and identifies himself with the Other, which is the best way to know him.

Source: *Diogenes*, No. 16 (Winter 1956), pp. 23–38. Reprinted by permission.

This is not to say that the Negro is traditionally devoid of reason, as one would have me believe. But his reason is not discursive; it is synthetic. It is not antagonistic, but sympathetic. This is another path to knowledge. Negro reason does not impoverish things. It does not mold them into rigid categories, eliminating the juices and the sap; it flows into the arteries of things, espouses all their contours and comes to rest in the living core of the real. White reason is analytical through use. Negro reason is intuitive through participation.

This describes the black man's sensitivity, his emotional power. Gobineau defined the Negro as "the most energetic creature seized with artistic emotion." For what strikes the Negro is less the appearance of an object than its profound reality, its surreality; less its sign than its meaning. Water enchants him because it flows, fluid and blue, particularly because it washes, and even more because it purifies. Sign and meaning express the same ambivalent reality. However, the stress is on meaning, which is the significance—no longer utilitarian, but moral, *mystique* of the real—a symbol. It is significant that contemporary scientists themselves affirm the primacy of intuitive knowledge through sympathy. "The finest emotion we can feel is a mystical one. In it resides the seed of all art and of all true science."

It is this physiopsychology of the Negro that explains his metaphysics and, moreover, his social life, of which literature and art are but one aspect. For African-Negro social life depends, according to Father Placide Tempels, upon a totality of concepts logically coordinated and motivated. This same missionary states that those whom the Europeans call the "primitives" live more than they themselves do "by ideas and according to ideas."

At the heart of the system, giving it light as the sun lights our world, is existence, that is to say, life. This is the supreme good and all of man's activity is but an attempt at expansion and expression of this vital force. The Negro identifies being with life, or, more precisely, with the vital force. His metaphysics is an existential ontology. As Father Tempels writes, "Being is that which possesses force," or even better: "Being is force." But this force is not static. A being is an unstable balance, always capable of reinforcing or weakening itself. In order to exist, man must achieve an expression of his individuality through the expansion and expression of his vital force. And this force, substratum of intellectual moral life, though immortal, is truly living and capable of growing only by coexisting, within man, with the body and the vital breath. The latter, made of matter, are perishable and they disintegrate after death.

But man is not the only being in the world. A vital power similar to his own animates every object endowed with sensitive characteristics, from God to a grain of sand. The Negro has established a hierarchy of forces. At the top, a single God, uncreated and creator: "he who has force, power through himself." After him come the ancestors, first of all the founders of the clan, the "similar-to-God." Then, going down the scale, we encounter the living, who are ordered, in turn, in accordance with custom, but mainly on the basis of age. Finally, at the bottom of the scale are the categories of animals, vegetables, and minerals. The same hierarchy exists in each of these.

This is the place to remark upon the unusual position of man, in the center of the system, in his quality of a person, in active existence, and capable of extending his being. For the universe is certainly a closed system of individual and distinct forces, but cohesive ones. Therefore, all of creation is centered upon man. To the extent that a being is a vital force, the ancestors, if they do not wish to be nonexistent, "entirely dead,"—this is a Bantu expression—must devote themselves to strengthening the life of the living man, which would enable them to participate in his life. As for inferior beings—animals, vegetables, and minerals—their sole goal in God's plan is to support the endeavors of the dead. They are instruments, not ends in themselves.

The merit of this existential ontology is to have enlightened, in turn, a harmonious civilization, and particularly an authentic religion. For what is a religion but, as its etymology claims, the bond that gives the universe its unity, which unites God to the Elymus and to the grain of sand? The ontology that we find here constitutes its dogma. As for the cult, which is the religion of actions, it is expressed in Negro Africa by sacrifices.

The head of the family is the one who offers the sacrifice. He is the priest, designated solely as being the oldest descendant of the common Ancestor. He is the natural mediator between the living and the dead. Closer to the dead, he lives intimately with them. His flesh is less flesh, his spirit more subtle, his word more powerfully persuasive: he is already a participant in the nature of the dead. The sacrifice is principally a contact with the Ancestor, a dialogue of thou and me. One shares with him the sustenance whose existential strength will give him the feeling of life. And communion extends to identification so that, by an inverse movement, the Ancestor's strength flows into the sacrificer and into the multitude which he incarnates. The sacrifice is the most typical illustration of the general law of the interaction of the vital forces of the world.

If we examine the natural aspect of the unitary order of the world, society, we will find that the family is its simplest component, the basic cell. Indeed, African-Negro society is formed by concentric circles growing wider and wider and rising gradually above each other, overlapping and shaped according to the category of the family itself. The tribe includes several families and the kingdom several tribes. But what is this family? It is the clan, the ensemble of the people, living or dead, who have an ancestor in common. This ancestor, himself a genius and "similar-to-God," is the link that connects God with men. His life often appears in the form of a totemic myth, occasionally connected with an astral myth. Hence the importance of the animal in Negro cosmogony. The Ancestor received vital force from God and his eternal vocation is to increase it. As we see, the aim of the family is to perpetuate a patrimony of vital force which increases and becomes intensified as it manifests itself to living bodies, to more and more numerous and prosperous existing beings. The family appears as a microcosm, an image of the universe which is reflected in and extended to the tribe and the kingdom. The King is but the father of "the-largest-family"; he is the descendant of "the-Leader-of-the-Tribes."

The family, the tribe, and the kingdom are not the only communitarian organisms that simultaneously bind and sustain the Negro. Besides these, a whole network of organisms exists, whose interests and activities cut across others. There are the age fraternities, a species of friendly societies into which the generations are divided; the corporations of trades and the brotherhoods with secret rites. These play a social, even a political, and, particularly, a religious role. Actually, all these organisms have a religious basis among people for whom a division between the sacred and the profane, between the political and the social, is a rare and belatedly acquired fact.

Literature and art are, quite naturally, integrated into the social activities sustained by religious feelings. A Westerner finds it difficult to understand the place that these occupy in the African-Negro calendar. They take up not merely a Sunday or "theatrical evenings" but in the Sudan, for example, the eight months of the dry season. During this time the people are entirely preoccupied with their relations with the Others: geniuses, ancestors, members of the family, tribe, or kingdom—even strangers. Celebrations follow celebrations and death itself is an occasion for festivity, for the best of celebrations: the festivity of the harvest and of sowing time; births, initiations, marriages, funerals; corporation and brotherhood festivities. And every evening tales are told around the hearth; there are dances, songs, gymnastic games, dramas, and comedies, illuminated by the tall flames. And works extolling the marriage of man with the land constitute another kind of story and poetry. So do songs of work, peasant songs, songs of boatmen and of shepherds. For in Negro Africa, as we shall see, all literature, all art is poetry.

Then there is always the matter of establishing relations either with the legendary totemic ancestors or with the mythical geniuses; the genius often has something of the star as well as of the animal, and the legends deepen to become a myth. Significant in this connection is the festival of initiation which is begun by numerous and continuing sacrifices. This is an initiation into cosmogonical myths, into legends and tribal customs and, more specifically, into the knowledge that a poem, a song, a play, a masked dance might give; it takes place to the primordial accompaniment of the rhythmic tam-tam. It is then that the grain dies in order to spring up again, that the child dies within himself to be reborn an adult, to become the Initiator and the Ancestor. This is a religious, animistic existentialism. The Other—adult, Ancestor, genius, or God—far from being an obstacle, is a prop, a source of vital force. In this confrontation of the me and the Thou there is no conflict but only peaceful agreement, no non-realization, but a greater realization of the individual essence.

And so literature and art are not separable from men's generic activities, particularly from the artisans' techniques. These are the most effective expressions of their activities. Let us remember Laye's father in *Enfant noir,* forging a golden jewel. The prayer he recites, for it is more a prayer than a poem, the praise that the *griot* sings as he works at the gold, the blacksmith's dance as he finishes his work—all these—poem and song and dance—plus the gestures of the artisan, round out the work of art and make a masterpiece of it. These arts, in the general sense of the world, appearing in the same perspective, are bound up with one another. Thus, for example, sculpture could not realize its goal without the charm of the dance and of the song-poem. Look at the man whom *Nyamié* incarnates, the Genius-Sun of the *Baoulé,* under the mask of the Ram. See him dance with the gestures of a ram to the rhythm of the orchestra, while the chorus sings a poem about the Genius's gesture. We have, here and there, a functional art. In this last example the masked dancer must identify himself with the Genius-Sun-Ram and, as the sacrificer, cause his strength to flow over the audience that participates in this drama.

There is another characteristic of the poem (once again, I mean by "poem" any work of art): it is created by everyone and for everyone. Of course there are professionals in literature and in art: in the countries of the Sudan, there are the *griots,* who are at once historiologists, poets, and story-tellers; in the countries of Guinea and of the Congo there are the civil sculptors of the princely courts who wear adzes on their sleeves as insignia of honor. Everywhere we find the blacksmith, that polytechnician of magic and of art, the first artist, according to a *dogon* myth, who, using the rhythmic beat of the tam-tam, makes rain fall from the sky. But alongside of these professionals there are the people, the anonymous masses who sing, dance, carve, and paint. The initiation is the black African school where man, emerging from infancy, assimilates himself to the sciences of the tribe, the techniques of literature and of art. Furthermore, the reader will have observed from the two examples I have cited that any manifestation of art is collective, for everyone's benefit, and with everyone's participation.

Because they are functional and collective, African-Negro literature and art are committed. This is their third general characteristic. They commit the person—and not only the individual—by and through the collectivity, in the sense that they are techniques of essentialization. They involve him in a future which from then on will become the present for him, the integrating part of his ego. This is why the African-Negro work of art is not, as has often been said, an imitation of an archetype that has been repeated a thousand times over. Of course there are similar subjects, each of which expresses a vital force. But the variety of the performance, attuned to individual temperament and circumstance, is what is most arresting. To repeat, then, the artisan-poet is fixed, and he involves along with himself *his* ethnic character, *his* history, and *his* geography. He uses the materials he has at hand and the daily events of which his life is composed. And yet he rejects the anecdote for the reason that it does not commit the individual, being devoid of meaning. Both painter and sculptor will, on occasion, make use of tools or materials imported from Europe. They will not hesitate to portray the machine —pride of the West; they will even go so far as to clothe an ancestral genius in the European manner. In the new society, enlightened by the spirit of the Colonial Pact, the story-teller will give money its rightful place, the first, as the incarnation of evil. Because he is committed, the artisan-poet is not concerned about creating a work for all eternity. A work of art is perishable. If one preserves the spirit and style one can readily duplicate an early work by modernizing it as soon as it becomes dated or destroyed. In other words, in Negro Africa, "art for art's sake" does not exist. All art is social. The *griot* who sings about noblemen at war sings all the louder and shares in their victories. When he chants about the acts of a legendary hero it is the history of his people he is describing in his own language; he is restoring to them the divine profundity of the myth. Even fables teach us a lesson over and beyond the laughter and the tears they evoke. They are one of the essentials of social equilibrium because of the dialectics they express. Beneath the figures of the Lion, the Elephant, the Hyena, the Crocodile, the Hare, the Old Woman, we read clearly and perceive our own social structures and our passions —the good as well as the bad. Sometimes these fables symbolize resistance to our elders, right opposed to brutal force, or perhaps acquiescence in the order of the universe, to the will of the Ancestors and of God. And the *Wolof* concludes, "It was thus that the fable went and threw itself into the sea. The first one to smell its aroma will go to paradise." Aromas of Negro wisdom!

However, one would completely fail to understand the essence of African-Negro literature and art if one conceived of them as being solely utilitarian or if one believed that the African Negro had no sense of beauty. Some ethnologists and art critics have claimed that the words "beauty" and "beautiful" are absent from the African-Negro languages. Quite the contrary. The truth is that the African Negro associates beauty with goodness and especially with efficaciousness. For example, in the *Wolof* of Senegal the words *tar* and *rafet,* "beauty" and "beautiful" are usually applied to men. In regard to works of art, the *Wolof* will use the qualifying terms *dyeka, yèm, mat,* which I would translate as: "which is suitable," "which is worthy of," "which is perfect." Here too beauty is *functional.* The beautiful mask, the beautiful poem, is one which inspires a desired emotion in the public: sadness, joy, hilarity, terror. The word *baxai* (goodness) is significant; it is used by young dandies to designate a beautiful young girl, as if for them beauty is "a promise of happiness." A kind act may also be designated as "beautiful."

If a certain poem produces an effect it is because it finds an echo in the minds and sensitivity of the listeners. That is why the *Peuls* define a poem as: "Words pleasing to the heart and to the ear." But although for both the African Negro and the European "the principal rule is to please," the two do not find pleasure in the same things In Greco-Roman aesthetics, which survived in Western Europe until the end of the nineteenth century, the Middle Ages excepted, art is an "imitation of nature," or, if you will, "a corrected imitation." In black Africa it is an explanation and knowledge of the world, tha is to say, a sensitive participation in the reality that sustains the universe, in the surreality, or, to be more precise, in the vital forces that animate the universe. The European derives pleasure from recognizing the world in the reproduction of an object designated by the term "subject," while the African Negro's pleasure resides in knowing the world intensely through imagery and rhythm. In the European, the thread of the senses leads to the heart and to the head; in the African Negro it leads to the heart and to the stomach, to the very root of life. The Ram's mask pleases the spectator because it incarnates the Genius-Sun in a plastic and rhythmic language.

Imagery and rhythm are the two fundamental characteristics of the African-Negro style. Let us speak of imagery first. But before so doing we must take a moment for a brief analysis of African-Negro languages and try to understand their nature and function. We will then be better able to comprehend the value of African-Negro imagery.

The word seems to us to be the major tool of thought, of emotion, and of action. There is no thought, no emotion, without verbal expression; there is no free action without a thought-out plan. And this is all the more true among people who, for the most part, scorn the written word. The power of the word in black Africa is in the spoken word: the verb is the finest expression of vital force, of a human being in all his plenitude. God created the world by use of the verb, as we shall soon see. In the existing person the word is the animated and animating breath of sound. It possesses magic virtue, realizes the law of participation, and creates the participant through its intrinsic virtue. Moreover, all other arts are but particular aspects of the major art of the word. Standing before a painting which consisted of a network of red and white geometric forms depicting birds singing in a tree beneath a rising sun, the artist explained it thus: "There are wings, song; those are birds . . ."[1]

What marks the African-Negro languages is, first of all, richness of vocabulary. There are ten, sometimes twenty words to denote an object, depending upon how it changes form, weight, volume, or color. There are just as many words to describe an action, depending upon whether it is single or multiple, weak or intense, beginning or ending. In *Peul*, nouns are divided into twenty-one neuter genders. Classification is at times based on their semantic value, or other times on their phonetic value, or again, on the grammatical category to which they belong. But it is the verb that is still the most significant. In *Wolof*, by using suffixes, one can construct on the same root more than twenty verbs which vary in their meanings; one can also con-

---

[1] José Rédinha, *Paredes pintadas da lunda*, Estampa 17 (Lisbon: 1953).

struct at least as many derivative nouns. While contemporary Indo-European languages stress the abstract notion of time, African-Negro languages emphasize the aspect, the concrete manner in which a verbal action occurs. In other words, the latter are essentially concrete languages. The words are always pregnant with imagery; the value of their meaning appears beneath their value as signs.

African-Negro imagery is therefore not imagery-equation but imagery-analogy, surrealist imagery. The African Negro despises the straight line and the false "proper word." Two and two do not make four but "five," as the poet Aimé Césaire says. The object does not signify what it represents but what it suggests, what it creates. The elephant is force; the spider, prudence; horns are the moon and the moon is fecundity. Any representation is imagery, and imagery, I repeat, is not equation but symbol, ideogram. It is not only imagery-form but the very matter—stone, earth, copper, or fiber—or even more than that, line and color. Any language that is not inventive is tiresome. Furthermore, the African Negro does not understand such language. Imagine the astonishment of the white people who first discovered that the "natives" understood neither their pictures nor even the logic of their speeches!

I have spoken about surrealist imagery, but the reader will have guessed that African-Negro surrealism is different from European surrealism. The one is empirical, the other mystical and metaphysical. André Breton writes in *Signe ascendant:* "The poetic analogy," meaning European surrealist analogy, "differs basically from the mystical analogy in that it in nowise presupposes, behind the framework of the visible world, an invisible universe that tends to manifest itself. It is entirely empirical in its application." On the contrary, the Negro surrealist analogy presupposes and manifests the hierarchized universe of vital forces.

Power of imagery, power of the word! For example, in Dahomey among the *Fons,* at every noteworthy event of his reign the king would invent a rhymed phrase, the most important word of which would constitute a new noun. "The pineapple that laughed at lightning." And the word and the pineapple would be inscribed everywhere, despotically, constituting an image: in wood, clay, gold, bronze, ivory; on the throne, the headdress, the scepter, and the palace walls.

In African-Negro poetry it is quite plain that the abstract word is rarely encountered. There is no need to comment upon imagery in this regard; the listeners are endowed with double vision. In sculpture, certain masks achieve an exemplary type of suggestion. One of these is the mask of the Genius-Moon-Bull among the *Baoulés.* Here we see the face of a man with a bearded chin, the horns and ears of a bull (sometimes the horns are replaced by a crescent moon), birds that peck at the forehead or at the horns of plenty; this is a perfect example of the image that creates over and beyond the world of appearances. The more an image is unreal, surreal, the more it expresses, as Breton says, "the interdependence of two objects of thought fixed on different planes, over which the logical functioning of the mind is not apt to build any bridge," and the stronger is the image. And African-Negro painting, so much misjudged, does not escape this law. Let us go back to Impression 17 of *Paredes pintadas de lunda*, referred to above. Its power of suggestion lies in the contrasting colors, white and red on a brown-black background; its exceptional geometrical shapes, squares, ovals, and angles; all this to depict birds singing as the sun rises. Even the music is a texture of imagery. For the primitive role of music in black Africa is not that of a concert, of oral enchantment, but rather to accompany the poem or the dance, that dynamic sculpture. Last year on the Ivory Coast I saw the Genius-Sun-Ram dance. The dancer expressed the sacred fury of the Ram by his dance steps and the orchestra expressed it in musical phrases. And this is also true of the narration—myth, legend, tale, or fable—even proverb and riddle. From the very fact that it represents learning, African-Negro narration naturally assumes the form of a parable, of an image moving in time and in space. "Once upon a time," "Once, a long, long time ago,"—this is not only the way myths and legends begin, but fables as well. In a fable the animal is rarely totemic. Rather it represents such or such a person whom everyone in the village knows quite well: the tyrannical and stupid leader, or the good and wise man, or the young champion of justice, Fatou, the Orphan. "Once upon a time," and the audience responds, "As usual." The story and the fable are interwoven with the events of the day because African-Negro ontology is existential. There is no place in it for the merely anecdotal or the "slice of life" type of story. Facts are imagery. They do not serve as good examples. This explains the charm of the narration, its rapid progression, its material improbabilities, and the absence of psychological explanations.

This imagery, however, produces no effect upon the African Negro if it is not rhythmic. Rhythm here is of the same substance as imagery. It rounds out imagery by unifying into a single entity both sign and meaning, flesh and spirit. The distinction that I make between the two elements is an artificial one and I do so only for the sake of clarification. In the music that accompanies a poem or a dance the rhythm is as much a part of the imagery as the melody. It is this rhythm in the mask of the Genius-Moon-Bull which permits a substitution of the image and it has the same symbolic value: crescent moon in place of the horns of plenty in place of the birds.

What is rhythm? It is the architectural structure of our being, the internal dynamism that gives us form, the network of undulations that Others receive from us, the pure expression of vital force. Rhythm is the vibrant shock, the power which, through our senses, lays hold of the very roots of our being. It expresses itself by the most material, the most sensual means: lines, colors, volume, in architecture, sculpture, and painting; stresses in poetry and in music, movements in the dance. But, having done this, it channels all that is concrete into intellectual spirit. For the African-Negro rhythm illuminates the spirit so that it becomes embodied in sensuality. The African dance disclaims bodily contact. Yet look at the dancers. While their lower limbs are agitated by most sensual movements, their heads partake of the serene beauty of masks, of the dead.

Once again, we see the primacy of the word. It is rhythm that lends it its full effectiveness, that transforms it into the verb. It was God's verb, that is to say the rhythmic word that created the universe. Furthermore, it is the poem that best instructs us on the nature of African-Negro rhythm. Rhythm is not born of the alternations of long and short syllables; it is created solely by the alternations of stressed and weak syllables, by the alternations of quick and slow tempos. This is a matter of rhythmic versification. Poetry exists when, during the same interval of time, the stressed syllable is repeated. But the essential rhythm is not created by the word but by the percussion instruments which accompany the human voice, or, to be more exact, by those percussion instruments that beat out the basic rhythm. This is a polyrhythmic beat, a kind of rhythmic counterpoint. And one is thus spared that mechanical regularity of the word, which makes for monotony. The poem, then, seems to have an architectural structure, a mathematical formula based upon unity in diversity. The following is the word-rhythm of two of the *Wolof* poems selected at random.[2]

a)	24 00	b)	32 31	32 31
	24 00		32 31	32 31
	44 00		22 31	22 31
	44 00		32 21	
	43 00		32 31	
	43 00		32 21	

[2] Cf. *"Langage et poésie nègre-africaine"* in *Poésie et langage* (Brussels: Editions de la Maison du Poète).

As we can see, the basic rhythm in the first case is 4444 and in the second, 3333. In both cases the verse is a tetrameter. The public often takes part in the poetic recital, and when this occurs we have two groups of rhythms. This enables the two star performers, the narrator and the leader of the tam-tams, to yield completely to their inspiration, to increase the off-beats and the syncopation, relying confidently upon the basic rhythm. For this monotonous, basic rhythm, far from hindering inspiration, is really a necessary condition for it. There are other elements of rhythm, however, besides those that I have described. There is the audience's clapping, the steps and gestures of the narrators and the tambourine players; one also observes certain figures of speech—alliterations, paronomasias, anaphoras—which are based upon a repetition of phonemes or sounds. These provide secondary rhythms and strengthen the effect of the whole. Finally, the poet uses many descriptive words, the importance of which has been explained by de la Vergne de Tressan. He tells us that these words, composed of onomatopoeia, constitute at times as much as one-third of the African-Negro vocabulary.

The "recitation in prose" also partakes of the grace of rhythm. In black Africa there is no fundamental difference between prose and poetry. A poem is merely more markedly and evenly rhythmic. It is readily recognizable because a percussion instrument always accompanies the recitation of a poem. A sentence can become a poem merely by stressing its rhythm; this is an expression of the tension of a being: the "being" of the being. It seems that "Once, a long, long time ago," all recitations were quite rhythmic, were poetry, in fact. During less ancient times, the story was still narrated but with a more monotonous intonation, and the subject-matter was pitched on a higher plane: it was part of a religious ceremony. Today we have the tale, even in the form of a fable, which is its most unsacrilegious form, still rhythmic, but not as markedly so. In the first place, the dramatic interest is not as carefully contrived. To be more precise, a careful manipulation of dramatic interest does not consist in proscribing repetition, as is done today in European story-telling. On the contrary, dramatic interest stems from repetition—repetition of a fact, a gesture, a song, of words that create the leitmotiv. But almost always a new element is introduced, a variation in the repetition, unity amid diversity. It is this new element that points up the dramatic progression. In other words, prose recitation does not scorn figures of speech based upon the repetition of phonemes, nor of descriptive words. Moreover, the structure of the African-Negro sentence is naturally rhythmic. For while Indo-European languages employ a logical subordinating syntax, African-Negro languages tend more readily to use an intuitive syntax of coordination and juxtaposition. And in propositions of approximately equal length the words are formulated in groupings, each one of major importance. As for rhythm, music is bound up with the word and with the dance, and of course more with the poem than with the dance. Rhythm, for the African Negro, is the element which best characterizes the poem. In the Senegalese languages the same word, *woi* in *Wolof*, *kim* in *Sérère*, *yimre* in *Peul*, denotes the finest expression of song and poetry: the ode. In any case, a poem is not complete unless it is sung or at least given rhythm by the accompaniment of a musical instrument. And the prose of the public crier becomes solemn and acquires authority because of the beat of the tam-tam. In African-Negro music, as has often been said, rhythm dominates melody. As I have said before, this is because the purpose of music is less to enchant the listener than to reinforce the word, to make it more effective. Hence the important role of rhythm, of sudden low tones, inflections, and vibrati; this shows a preference for expression rather than for harmony.

The ethnological, religious, and social values of African-Negro sculpture have been greatly emphasized during the last few years. And yet those writers and artists who, at the beginning of the century, stressed the aesthetic value of rhythm were not wrong. Let us merely leaf through certain volumes in which African-Negro sculpture is reproduced; for example, Carl Kjersmeier's book: *Centres de style de la sculpture nègre-africaine* (Paris, Copenhagen), pausing at Figure 48, which shows a feminine statuette of the *Baoulé*. Two soft melodies sing an alternating song here. Ripe fruits of the womb. The chin and the knees, the rump and the calves are also fruits. Neck, arms, limbs—columns of black honey. In another volume the *fang* statuette of the *Gabon* again offers us fruits—womb, navel, knees—in contrast to the curved cylinder of the bust, the thighs, and the calves of the legs. Let us next look at the first volume, at this upper portion of a *bambara* mask that represents the antelope. Music of the horns and ears, anti-melody of the tail and neck. And the hair of its mane springs from the sculptor's imagination. As André Malraux writes in *Les Voix du Silence*, "The African mask is not the rendering of a human expression, it is an apparition. . . ." In it the sculptor does not geometrize some phantom he does not know, he creates him by his geometry. His mask exerts its influence less because of its resemblance to man than because of its lack of resemblance. Masks of animals are not animals; the mask of the antelope is not an antelope but antelope-spirit, and it is its style that creates this "spirit." By style I mean its rhythm.

Rhythm is to be found again in African-Negro painting. The present-day painters of Potopoto and of Elizabethville have begun to convince the attentive observer that this is so. They are merely continuing a very ancient tradition. We know that African-Negro sculpture is often painting as well. Yet in the last twenty years the mural painters of black Africa have been discovered, reproduced, and commented upon. Rhythm here is not marked by lines that separate light from shadow, it is not arabesque as in European classical painting. Actually, the African Negroes use flat colors that do not give the effect of shadow. Rhythm is created here as elsewhere by repetition, often at regular intervals, of a line, a color, a figure, a geometrical form; and, strangely enough, by a contrast of colors. Usually the painter places figures in light colors on a dark background, or vice versa, and this gives the impression of space or of time gone by, which lends the painting a feeling of depth. The design and the coloring of the figures correspond less to reality than to the profound rhythm of the objects. Two examples will suffice as illustration. The upper part of a painting contains a frieze that portrays the sumptuous procession of a prince. It consists of six people who are moving from left to right. Beginning at the right, one encounters three members of the procession and two porters carrying a kind of stretcher on their shoulders upon which the prince is reclining. Then, bringing up the rear of the procession is the fourth member of the retinue. The background of the painting is light brown. The figures are painted in the three traditional colors of black Africa: white, black, and red. The six people in the procession all wear white headdresses, black tunics, red belts, white trousers, and black shoes. But the monotony of this basic rhythm is broken by the introduction of secondary rhythms. The two porters wear tunics dotted with white while the other members of the procession merely have a row of white buttons on their black tunics. The exception is the leader of the procession whose tunic has no buttons at all. One of the porters is wearing leggings similar to the ones worn by other members of the procession while the second porter is wearing low shoes. Two men, one of whom heads the procession while the other brings up the rear, carry sticks, but one stick is black, the other white. Finally, there are two birds painted on the bottom of the frieze, one of which is black with white dots, like the porter's tunic, and the other which is white, like the trousers and headdress of the men in the procession.

Now let us look at "Painting 54A" that portrays plants in pots.

The two figures are painted in two colors, blue and red, on a straw-colored background. Everything is blue and red—the stems, the leaves, the flowers, the pots—and placed symmetrically in almost geometrical form, accompanied by secondary rhythms. Decorative paintings, one might say. I would answer, African-Negro paintings, rhythmic paintings. And this is all the more significant since the examples I have chosen have felt the impact of European influences.

We must conclude. Here, then, is the African Negro for whom the world exists by virtue of the act reflected upon him. He does not state that he thinks; he feels that he feels, he feels his existence, he feels himself. Because he feels himself, he feels the Other; and because he feels the Other, he goes toward him on the rhythm of the Other, in order to know Him and his world. It is this soaring of the vital force that the religious and social life of the African Negro expresses, of which literature and art are the most effective tools. And the poet cries out: *"Eia!* Perfect tour of the world and close concord."[3]

You will tell me that the spirit of civilization and the laws of African-Negro culture as I have described them are true not only of the African Negro but of other peoples as well. I do not deny it. Every people expresses, in its visage, the various traits of its human condition. But I declare that the totality of these traits are nowhere to be found as balanced, as bathed in light, as in black Africa. Nowhere else has rhythm reigned as despotically. Nature planned things well in seeing to it that every people, every race, every continent would cultivate with special pleasure certain of man's virtues. This is precisely man's originality. And if one should add that African-Negro culture is as like that of ancient Egypt or of the Dravidian and Oceanian peoples as two sisters, I would answer that ancient Egypt was African and that black blood flows abundantly in the veins of the Dravidians and the Oceanians.

If there is a lesson to be learned from this study, it is not up to me to point it out to the men of the West. I will only say that to admire Negro art for the wrong reasons is to run the risk of not benefiting from it at all.

My concluding remarks I would like to address to the Negroes. The African-Negro spirit of civilization consciously or unconsciously animates the finest Negro artists and writers of our day, whether they are African or American. If they are aware of this and are inspired by African-Negro culture, they rise to international levels;

[3] Aimé Césaire, *Cahier d'un retour au pays natal.*

if they turn their backs on Mother Africa, they degenerate and become insipid, like Antaeus, who needed the support of the earth in order to leap back to heaven. This does not mean that Negro artists and writers of today must turn their backs on the real and refuse to interpret the social reality of their environment, their race, their nation or class. On the contrary, we have seen that the spirit of African-Negro civilization has embodied itself in the most current of daily reality. But this reality it always transcends in order to express the meaning of the world.

The literary and artistic history of Europe is proof that we must remain faithful to this spirit. After the failure of Greco-Roman aesthetics, at the end of the nineteenth century, Western writers and artists turned to Asia—above all to Africa—at the end of their searchings. Thus they have been able to legitimize their discoveries and confer a human value upon them. This is not the moment one should choose to betray, along with black Africa, our reasons for living.

CHEIKH ANTA DIOP

Cheikh Anta Diop, who was born in the town of Diourbel, Senegal, in 1923, has become one of the most controversial of recent African historians. Having completed his secondary education in Senegal, he went to France after the Second World War and undertook his advanced studies at the University of Paris. There he offered as his doctoral thesis what has since become his best-known work, *Nations nègres et culture*. Because of its deviation from established canons of historical interpretation and detachment, the thesis was rejected but subsequently was published. At the suggestion of his university professors, Diop undertook another dissertation and received his doctorate in 1960. In the following year he returned to Senegal where he assumed a position at the *Institut fondamental de l'Afrique noire*.

Nations nègres et culture is both a reassessment of the African past and a defiance cast at Western scholarship. In an attempt to refute the prevalent Hamitic myth of the past, Diop argues that Pharaonic Egypt was black populated, its civilization a black African one. The "white" myth of Egypt, he insists, became prevalent with European imperialism, beginning with the Napoleonic invasion of Egypt and Champillon's interpretations of Egyptology.

Diop has mustered considerable data to sustain his thesis and has particularly reworked ancient Greek sources to prove that Egyptians were black. As he delves into cultural differences, he contrasts the European world, which has become both materialistic and bellicose, with the African world, which is more spiritual and harmonious in structure.

Diop's history is engaged history, history written with a present-minded purpose. It is his intention to prove that, through Egyptian civilization, Africa has made the oldest and one of the most significant contributions to world culture. Not only does he thus assert the unity of precolonial Africa, but he points also to the justifiable pride contemporary Africans can have in it.

FURTHER READING: Erica Simon. "La Négritude et les problèmes culturels de l'Afrique contemporaine," *Présence africaine*, No. 47, 1963, pp. 145–172.

Cheikh Anta Diop

From *Nations nègres et culture*

The general problem confronting African history is this: how to recombine effectively, through meaningful research, all the fragments of the past into a single ancient epoch, a common origin which will reestablish African continuity. It is therefore necessary to demonstrate that a serious appreciation of the unanimous evidence offered by the scholars of antiquity to the effect that the Ethiopians and Egyptians were Negro—as were all the other autochthonous peoples of Africa—provides further clarification of an aspect of history which really was obscured only in the last century with the apogee of imperialism. If the Ancients were not victims of a mirage, it should be easy enough to draw up another series of arguments and proofs for the union of the history of Ethiopian and Egyptian societies with that of the rest of Africa. Thus combined, these histories would lead to a properly patterned past in which it would be seen that Ghana rose in the interior of the continent at the moment of Egyptian decline, just as the Western European empires were born with the decline of Rome.

* * *

Egypt had lost its independence over a century before the visit of Herodotus. Conquered by the Persians in 525, it continued to be dominated by foreigners: after the Persians, it was the Macedonians with Alexander the Great, the Romans with Julius Caesar (50 B.C.), the Arabs in the seventh century, the Turks in the sixteenth century, the French with Napoleon, and then the English at the end of the nineteenth century.

The cradle of civilization for over 10,000 years, and at a time when the rest of the world was still plunged in barbarism, Egypt, destroyed by these successive invasions, no longer played an important political

---

Source: *Nations nègres et culture* by Cheikh Anta Diop, published by *Présence africaine*, Paris (1954), pp. 15–16, 29–31, 249–250, 251–253. Reprinted by permission of the publisher. Selections translated by the editor.

role but nevertheless still long continued to initiate the young Mediterranean peoples (Greeks and Romans among others) into the enlightenment of civilization. Throughout all of antiquity, she remained the classical land to which Mediterranean peoples came on pilgrimage so that they might drink at the oldest scientific, religious, moral, and social mainspring mankind had acquired.

As a result new civilizations were successively erected around the periphery of the Mediterranean. These civilizations, benefiting from the many advantages provided by the geographical configuration of the Mediterranean, the best situated crossroads in the world, particularly evolved toward a materialist and technical development, which originated in the materialist genius of the Indo-Europeans, the Greeks and the Romans.

The pagan inspiration which animated this Graeco-Roman civilization died out around the fourth century. Two new factors, Christianity and the barbarian invasions, intruded on the already old terrain of Western Europe to give birth to a new civilization, that one which today manifests in its turn the symptoms of decay. This latter civilization which, thanks to the uninterrupted contacts among the various peoples, inherited all the technical progress of humanity, found itself in the fifteenth century sufficiently equipped technically to launch the discovery and conquest of the world.

Thus, with the fifteenth century, the Portuguese approached Africa by way of the Atlantic Ocean, and, in so doing, established the first modern Western contacts with Africa, contacts which were henceforth uninterrupted.

What did the Portuguese then find at this other extremity of Africa? What were the populations encountered; were they there from time immemorial or had they recently migrated? What was their cultural level, the degree of their social and political organization? In a word, what was the state of their civilization? What impressions did the Portuguese have of these populations? What ideas were they able to form of their intellectual capacities and of their technical aptitudes? What would be the nature of the social contact which would henceforth exist between Europe and Africa? In what fashion did this contact constantly evolve?

The answers to these different questions will provide the complete explanation of the present myth of the primitive Negro.

To reply to these different questions, it is indispensable to go back to Egypt at the moment when it fell under the yoke of foreigners.

The distribution of the Negroes on the African continent seems to have passed through two principal phases.

It is commonly admitted that around 7000 B.C. the desiccation of the Sahara was completed. Equatorial Africa was probably still a zone of forests too dense to attract men. At the same time the last Negroes who lived in the Sahara had probably left to emigrate toward the Upper Nile, with the exception, perhaps, of a few isolated pockets cast on the rest of the continent because of migration either southward or northward. Perhaps the former group encountered the autochthonous Negro population in the Upper Nile region. Whatever the case, it was from the progressive adaptation to new conditions of life which nature had assigned these different Negro populations that the oldest example of civilization the world has known was born. This civilization, called Egyptian in our times, developed for a long time in its original cradle, then slowly descended the length of the Nile Valley to end up by spreading out around the basin of the Mediterranean. The cycle of civilization, thus established, was the longest in history, probably lasting some 10,000 years, which is a fair estimate between the long chronology (Herodotus and Manethon, following the estimates of the Egyptian priests, situated the origins at 17,000 B.C.) and the short chronology of the Moderns who are obliged to admit that in 4245 B.C. the Egyptians had invented the calendar, an event which pre-supposed milennia of development in order to arrive at such calculations.

It can be readily appreciated that the Negroes during this long period could have once again spread progressively toward the interior of the continent, and formed the nuclei which then became the centers of continental civilization.

* * *

These African civilizations were to be more and more cut off from the rest of the world. They tended to live in isolation as a result of the enormous distance which separated them from the routes to the Mediterranean. When Egypt lost its independence, their isolation was complete.

Thereafter cut off from the foreign-invaded country, turning in on themselves in a geographic environment requiring a lesser effort of adaptation, benefiting from favorable economic conditions, the Negroes directed themselves toward their social, political, and moral development more than toward a speculative, scientific research which the environment not only did not justify, but also rendered impossible. Just as adaptation in the narrow fertile valley of the Nile required an intelligent technical knowledge of irrigation and dikes, of precise calculations to determine the floors of the Nile and to deduce their economic and social consequences; just as it was materially necessary to invent geometry in order to delimit property boundaries after the floods of the Nile had effaced them and also to settle the inhabitants; just as the long flat bands of terrain required the transformation of the paleonegretic hoe into the plow, drawn first by men, then by animals; just as all of this was indispensable for the material existence of the Negro in the Nile Valley, so also, all of these developments became superfluous in the new conditions of life in the interior of the continent.

His old equilibrium with his environment historically broken, the Negro found a new equilibrium, different from the first by the absence of a technology which was no longer of vital importance to his social, political, and moral organization.

Because the economic resources were assured by means which did not require perpetual inventions, the Negro progressively became disinterested in material progress.

* * *

It is impossible to insist on all that the world, and the Hellenic world in particular, owes to the Egyptian world. The Greeks only took over and occasionally developed, to some extent, Egyptian inventions. Because of their materialist tendencies the Greeks did this by stripping these inventions of the religious, the "idealist" covering which surrounded them. The rudeness of life in the Eurasian plains seems to have developed the materialist instinct of the people who lived there and, furthermore, to have forged moral values opposed to Egyptian moral values which derived from a relatively easy and peaceful collective sedentary life which instantly arose after the creation of a few social rules. Just as the Egyptians had a horror of theft, nomadism, and war, so these practices were considered as primary moral values in the Eurasian plains. Only the warrior fallen on the field of battle could enter Valhalla, Germanic paradise. Among the Egyptians the only dead person who could gain bliss at the Tribunal of Osiris was the one who could prove that he had never committed a sin and had been charitable toward the poor. This attitude was the opposite of the spirit of the razzia and of conquest which generally characterized the peoples of the North who were in some way chased from their naturally disinherited land. On the contrary, existence was so easy in the Valley of the Nile, a true flowing of life between two deserts, that the Egyptian had the tendency to believe that the benefits of nature fell on him from heaven. Thus he ended up by adoring the latter in the form of an All Powerful Being, Creator of all that exists, a dispenser of goodness. The Egyptians' primitive materialism—that is to say, his vitalism—henceforth became a materialism transposed to heaven, a metaphysical materialism, so to say.

On the contrary, the horizons of the Greek never went beyond material and visible man, conqueror of hostile nature. On earth, all gravitated around him: the supreme goal of man's art was exact duplication of himself. In "heaven," rather paradoxically, he alone was found with his earthly faults and weaknesses hidden under the guise of gods, who were indistinguishable from the mortals except for their physical strength. Thus when the Greek borrowed the Egyptian god, a god who was a true god in every sense of the word and endowed with all the moral perfections possible emanating from sedentary life, when the Greek borrowed this Egyptian god, he was incapable of understanding and preserving him except by reducing him to the level of man, by bringing him down to the human level. The borrowed Greek pantheon therefore simply became another humanity. It is this anthropomorphism, which was in this instance only an acute materialism, that characterized the Greek spirit.

* * *

Egypt was really the classical land to which two thirds of the Greek intellectuals and philosophers went to be schooled. In truth, it can be said that Alexandria, at the time of the Hellenistic period, was the intellectual center of the world, where all the Greek scholars now remembered were assembled. The fact cannot be sufficiently emphasized that these scholars were educated outside of Greece in Egypt itself.

Even Greek architecture had its roots in Egypt. As early as the XII dynasty, proto-doric columns (Tomb of Beni-Hasza) were noticeable.

The Graeco-Roman monuments are but miniatures when compared with the Egyptian. For instance, Notre-Dame of Paris, even with its towers, would have easily been placed within the hypostyle room of the Temple of Karnak; and even more easily so placed would have been the Greek Parthenon.

The genre of the fable, typically Negro . . . which consists of employing animals as characters was introduced into Greece by the Egyptian Negro Aesop, inspirer of the fables of La Fontaine.

Edgar Poe, in his "Some Words with a Mummy" *(New Unusual Tales)* provides a symbolic idea of the range of scientific and technical knowledge among the ancient Egyptians.

Herodotus had already received information from the mouth of ancient Egyptian priests which revealed the mathematical formula of the Great Pyramid.

* * *

The Egyptian origins of civilization and the extensive borrowing made from it by Greece being historically evident, it might be asked ... why, despite these facts, the historical emphasis is placed on the role played by Greece while that of Egypt is more frequently passed silently by.

The logic of this attitude can only be grasped by recalling the basic aspects of the question.

Because Egypt was a Negro country and the civilization developed there was due to the Negroes, any thesis trying to prove the contrary will be of no avail. The protagonists of such theses are hardly unaware of this fact. Thus it is wiser and surer to rob Egypt purely and simply and discretely of all its creations—and for the benefit of a people of truly white origin.

This false attribution of values from an Egypt qualified as white to a Greece equally white reveals a profound contradiction which is not the least of the proofs of the Negro origins of Egyptian civilization.

As one has seen, the man of color ... far from being incapable of technical creativity is the one who first did so in the person of the Negro and at a time when all the white races, plunged in barbarism, were only barely susceptible to civilization.

In stating that it was the ancestors of the Negroes, who today principally live in black Africa, who were the first to invent mathemathics, astronomy, the calendar, sciences in general, the arts, religion, agriculture, social organization, medicine, writing, architecture; who were the first both as architects and engineers (and not only as workers) to raise edifices of six million tons of stone (the Great Pyramid); who were those who constructed the Great Temple of Karnak, this forest of columns with its famous hypostyle room where Notre-Dame with its spires would be housed; who were those who sculpted the first colossal statues (colossus of Memnon, etc.)—in stating all of this, we are only stating the modest and strict truth which no one can now refute by arguments worthy of the name.

Henceforth the Negro must be capable of recovering the continuity of his national historical past. He must draw from it the moral lessons necessary to reconquer his place in the modern world, yet doing this without succumbing to the excess of a Nazism in reverse. For the civilization which he reclaims could have been created by any human race—insofar as one can speak of a race—which happened to be placed in such a favorable and unique original situation.

SAMUEL W. ALLEN

Samuel W. Allen, lawyer and poet who writes under the pseudonym Paul Vesey, is probably better known in Europe as a writer than in the United States. After studying both in the United States and France, he held several academic posts in the United States, and is currently professor of English at Boston University. His outstanding literary work is *Ivory Tusks*. Allen has actively participated in black literary circles: he knew Richard Wright when the latter was in Paris; he attended the Second Congress of Black Writers and Artists which was held in Rome in 1959; he has been one of the members of the advisory committee of the important Nigerian literary publication *Black Orpheus*.

Allen's essay on negritude was presented to the First Conference of Negro Writers, which was held in New York between February 28 and March 1, 1959, a conference which brought together an impressive group of black American authors and critics. Allen presented a French version of his paper the following month at the Second Congress of Black Writers and Artists.

The following selections have been revised by the author.

FURTHER READING: Guy Dickenberger. "Paul Vesey," *Black Orpheus*, No. 4 (October 1958), pp. 5–8.

Samuel W. Allen

From *Negritude and Its Relevance for the American Negro Writer*

In discussing the future direction of creative endeavor, it is least possible to be doctrinaire.[1] The creative effort appears to be in large measure a refusal to be bound, a breaking forth, a reaction to prescription. And all critical preoccupation with the future of any area of creative activity is apt to be proved vain, in error, and subject to reversal by the superior court of hindsight.

Turning, then, to negritude, we see that it has developed principally among the poets of African descent writing in the French language, including not only the poets of the African continent itself but also those of the Caribbean area, of Martinique, etc., who are also writing in French. Among these are Aimé Césaire, the late Jacques Roumain, Rene Depestre, Léon Damas, Laleau, Niger, and others who, remote from what they feel to be a lost homeland that exists in the nostalgic, collective memory, are more intense in their reaction to the estrangement of the African in Western society than the poets of the continent are.

In passing, we may note that this term, "negritude," is unsettling to many, perhaps because it puts into the realm of the explicit that which might more comfortably remain in the area of the implicit. The Negro is denied an acceptable identity in Western culture, and the term negritude focuses and carries with it the pejorative implications of that denial. The fact that it was possible for the term to

---

Source: Samuel Allen, *The American Negro Writer and His Roots* (New York: American Society of African Culture, 1960), pp. 9–10, 12–14, 16–19. Reprinted by permission.

[1] This paper was written in 1959 and, although minor revisions have been made, the landscape of that period is evident in its terminology and in the cast of its concern in dealing with the resistance, then much more uniform than now, to black affirmation. (Author's footnote.)

emerge in the literature is undoubtedly symbolic of the necessity of the development it represents. It is the latter with which we are principally concerned; what to call it, while important, is secondary.

The work of these poets of the Caribbean and of those of the continent—Léopold Senghor, David Diop, Birago Diop, and, among those writing in English, Efua Morgue, Dei Anang, Carey Thomas, Adeboye Babalola, has served and is serving to cast off the cultural imprint of colonial Europe; it is a type of reconnaissance in the formation of a new imaginative world free from the proscriptions of a racist West. Their creative activity reveals an effort toward a renewal of their lost organic vision of the universe, which is inextricably involved in, and as crucial as, the political and economic enfranchisement presently occurring. The African finds himself bound fast in the culture prison of the Western world, which has held him for centuries in derision and contempt; his poetic concern has been with his liberation from his prison, with the creation of a truer sense of identity, and with the establishment of his dignity as a man. This preoccupation led to the birth in the French language of the central concept of negritude, principally in the work of Léopold Senghor and Aimé Césaire. The term is not amenable to easy definition. It appears to serve in somewhat varying roles for those who employ it. It represents in one sense the Negro African poet's endeavor to recover for his race a normal self-pride, a confidence in himself shattered for centuries when the enslaver suddenly loomed in the village pathway; to recover a world in which he once again could have a sense of unashamed identity and an unsubordinate role. Jean-Paul Sartre wrote an excellent preface to Senghor's 1947 anthology of African poetry in the French language, and in this, he likened negritude to an African Eurydice, recovered by the song of Orpheus from Pluto. It is the African's lost beloved, his complete and ultimate self, his vision of the world, not the spirit of a culture in which he swells on sufferance or which holds him in veiled and unveiled disdain. It is not simply a goal to be accomplished, but rather, more functionally, an affective disposition. In Heidegger's existentialist term, it indicates the Negro's "being-in-the-world." Senghor points out that the negritude of a poem is less the theme than the style, its characteristic manner, the intensity of its passion, its rhythmic flow or the quality of its imagery, whether he writes of a ritual dance in Dahomey, of the Brittany seacoast, or of the nature of God and man. Negritude includes the characteristic impulses, traits, and habits which may be considered more markedly Negro African than white or European. It is thus something which the poet possesses in the wells of his being and simultaneously something which he is seeking to recover, to make manifest; and again it is a subjective disposition which is affirmed and which objectivizes itself in the poem.

Aimé Césaire writes:

> My negritude is not a rock, its deafness hurled against the clamor of the day
> My negritude is not a film of dead water on the dead eye of the earth
> My negritude is neither a tower nor a cathedral
> It plunges into the red flesh of the earth
> It plunges into the burning flesh of the sky
> It pierces the opaque prostration by its upright patience.

In these lines, Césaire emphasizes the dynamic quality of this concept; negritude is an act, an active becoming, a vital force patiently and stubbornly active in the earth and the sky and the elements. Amid the insufferable tensions of his estrangement, negritude is that area the poet has carved out for himself in the poem where he may live and dwell and have his true and absolute being:

> The words surpass themselves. It is indeed toward a sky and a land whose height and depth cannot be troubled. It is made of the old geography. Yet there now emerges at a certain level an area curiously breathable. At the gaseous level of the solid and liquid organism, white and black, night and day.

We should note that a common reaction among Americans—tutored in a society strongly egalitarian and integrationist in avowed direction and ideal, however derelict in deed—is one of surprise that the Negro African, who above all has been the victim of racial persecution, should affirm racial qualities. However, a consideration of the historical circumstances giving rise to its development tends to make clear its justification, and more, its necessity. The reaction to centuries of humiliation and contempt is not one of calm objectivity. The pendulum can only gradually achieve dead center. Each age, each people has its own historical necessity. In this connection, Sartre has used Hegelian concepts, which serve well here, to describe this movement. Negritude in African poetry is an anti-racist racism; it is the moment of negativity in reaction to the thesis of white supremacy. It is the antithesis in a dialectical progression which leads to an ultimate synthesis of a common humanity without racism. This is undoubtedly too neat a formula for the actual operation of the influences involved; yet it does provide a ready and roughly accurate framework for the comprehension of the conflicting tendencies at play here. We see, too, that these poets are deeply aware that man, ultimately, is man and that his race is an attribute, only, of his more basic membership in the human community. Jacques Romain gives particularly poignant testimony:

> Africa I guard your memory Africa
> you are in me as the shaft is in the wound
> as the guardian fetish in the center of the village
> make of me the stone of your sling
> of my mouth the lips of your sores
> of my knees the broken columns of your humiliation
>   and yet
> I wish to be only of your race
> fellow workers of every land.

We have considered this concept, this esthetic, this rebel to analysis—negritude—confining our remarks thus far to the work of African and French West Indian writers and the role negritude has played in their development. Let us consider briefly the possible relevance of this concept to the work of the American Negro writer or, to put it differently, its validity for a writer in our cultural situation.

I think it has a role. This is not necessarily so for all of us, the writer not being a soldier marching to command. He writes, when he writes most creatively, pursuant to his own individual and most deeply felt need. The racial accident of his birth may have little or only indirect influence on the thrust of his writing, although for a black writer in America this is difficult to imagine. It is probably true also that it was not by chance that this concept, negritude, originated among the poets rather than among those working in prose. Except for certain highly imaginative works, the novelist writes within a framework of what we term reality. He must in part concern himself with Plato's shadows—with plot and setting. His characters, unlike Orphan Annie, must grow up. He is constrained to a certain degree of reasonableness. The poet has probably a greater chance to penetrate, at once without apology and without a setting of the worldly state, to the deepest levels of his creative concern. And so, perhaps what we are saying may have greater applicability to poetry than to prose.

I think there is little disagreement that our cultural situation is substantially different from that of Amos Tutuola, of Efua Morgue of Ghana, of the Senegalese, resident of Paris since his university days, or of the Haitian or Jamaican writer. Our contact with Africa has been remote for centuries, and both the natural and the consciously directed impacts of the enslavement were to shatter the African cultural heritage. Further, the American Negro, uprooted from his homeland, has been subjected in a manner unparalleled among other peoples of African descent to the cultural imprint of a powerful, dominant majority in a strange and unfriendly land. The Ashanti, the Senegalese, the Yoruba were overwhelmed militarily and politically and subjected to a foreign culture; but they were on their home ground, and they retained the morale afforded by the mystic attachment to the soil of their ancestors. The colonizing European, though controlling, was a minority, and the African remained in large part Senegalese, Ashanti, Yoruba. And even in South Africa, the Zulu, uprooted and driven into the mines, remained upon his own continent. The West Indian, though like the Negro of the United States, captive and transplanted across the ocean, at least retained the advantage of numbers and an infrequency of contact with a ruling and relatively restrained elite. In contrast, the American Negro has undergone a physical and spiritual alienation without parallel in modern history. Overwhelmed militarily, uprooted and transplanted 3,000 miles from his native soil, he has been subjected for centuries to the close, daily cultural impress not only of a dominant elite but also of the lowest elements of what Claude McKay has termed a "cultural hell," created by a powerful, materialistic, and brutal frontier society, uncertain of its own identity and seeking to assure itself of status in part by the denial of status to its victims. Rightfully resentful of the privilege of the old world, our American society itself fell victim to a psychological complex of denigration—a complex which, it is perfectly patent today, has redounded to its own disadvantage in the assault upon the intellectual, in the rock-throwing at the egghead, in the triumph in America of a cultural mediocrity.

The question, then, is posed whether this unparalleled alienation and our partial entrance into what is termed the mainstream of American life precludes our exploration and affirmation of our identity as a minority of African descent and our recourse to the African heritage as a fructifying source of our creative endeavor. (And this, basically, has been the function of negritude—to serve as a means toward the achievement of a sense of full cultural identity and a normal self-pride within the cultural context.) Lest there be some confusion, it should be pointed out that we are dealing here not with the question of social segregation on the basis of race, but with an analysis of our cultural situation and an exploration of the aspects of our identity, which, though thwarted by the prevailing racial mores, may nonetheless be a fertile source of creative inspiration. It is evident that such an exploration is a necessity not only for the African but for the Afro-American as well.

There may be differences, as there were in the debate in Paris between Aimé Césaire and some of the American delegation, as to whether the American Negro is, or has been, subjected to a species of colonialism. The fact is he has felt himself to be in an alien, not a native, land, to plagiarize Willard Savoy and Richard Wright. He too feels about him as Countee Cullen says in "Heritage," a culture prison. The consequence of this feeling is evident to the observer. Henry Wallace, visiting the West Indies, noted what he felt to be a greater personal stature on the part of the West Indian. I have heard Mr. Killens say that Dorothy Dandridge was struck by the deep sense of assurance and quiet pride she found in the Senegalese. The psychologists Kardiner and Ovesey have recently traced the psychological profile of the American Negro in their book *The Mark of Oppression*. Dubose Heyward portrays the effect of this culture prison in *Porgy*, in which the hero, the American Negro, is symbolically a cripple, and in which the only man of full stature is the character who never in the course of the play experiences a confrontation with the all-powerful white authorities, and who refuses reasonably to conform and to make the best of the social pattern. He is the outlaw, the gambler, the near rapist, the murderer, who is symbolically named Crown.

Thus do we see the effect of the dominant cultural pattern. I think it a significant commentary upon the direction of that pattern that it is necessary, with perhaps some exceptions, to return to the nineteenth century to find among America's outstanding writers—in the great-souled Melville, in the mystic Thoreau, in the cosmic vision of Whitman—the spiritual dimension to comprehend and to transcend the fact of race in America.

When we consider, then, the nature of the role the Negro has occupied in America's cultural design, when we consider the materialistic stamp of America's contemporary contributions to man's cultural progress, it appears we should be wary of making too eager, too anxious, too precipitous a jump into what is termed the mainstream of that culture. That the Negro is an American is a fact of history. And though it may be true, as T. S. Eliot said, that the time-and-place social history of the artist is not necessarily his *significant* prior experience as far as his creative direction is concerned, yet it is probable that his creative effort will bear the strong imprint of his experience within his society. However, and this is the focal point of the discussion, it does the Negro writer a disservice to think of his work as a tributary to some major American stream, an attitude implicit in the frequent injunction to enter into the mainstream of American culture.

Hegel has somewhere said that the slave must not only break the chain; he must also shatter the image in both his and his former master's mind before he can truly become free. The mainstream of American arts and letters, it is obvious, falls woefully short of reflecting the Negro with dignity and with complete psychological integrity. To think merely of joining that stream or to think of our creative effort simply as part of that stream would mean to fall to a substantial degree under the influence of its direction and to perpetrate in part its cultural prototypes. (Here we should distinguish between a mastery of the content and techniques of a literature and the danger of a self-immolating submission to it.) It would be, and has proved in large measure in the Negro Renaissance of the twenties to be, a more fruitful approach for the American Negro to write out of his own felt need, looking to the creative sources of his inclination, defining himself in terms of the deeper wells of his being as he may discover them in the direction of his particular interests, talents, and emotional reactions. He should seek his inspiration in what life in this society has meant to *him* and, if he finds it seminal, in the history, mythology, and folklore of Africa, in the battles of Chaka, in Benin bronze, in the Bantu philosophy of vital force, forgetting for the time being the necessity of an American mainstream. There is small chance that the body of creative effort of the American Negro will not reflect his American experience. But it is only in an emphasis upon the development of his own identity in that experience that he will be able to make ultimately his fullest contribution to the whole, within and without the nation.

Because this culture prison to which we have referred has imposed a wall between him and his origins, it is to those origins that the artist is drawn to recover that lost fullness of self. Thus, for example, Amos Tutuola, author of the celebrated *Palm Wine Drinkard*, was able, by pursuing his own ancestral experience and developing his own style of expression, to create something totally divergent from current British literary trends. Though to a sophisticated London ear, his syntax may leave something to be desired, he has gone far toward creating an African mythology and resurrecting the magic of his

African heritage, which he undoubtedly would not have accomplished had he been more alert and responsive to English literary trends. Here in America, it was not in pursuit of a mainstream that Langston Hughes created something new under the literary sun when he contained on paper the haunting refrains of the blues. And, similarly, it was in a retreat to the sources of his own identity that James Weldon Johnson captured the beauty and the power of the Southern Negro preacher in *God's Trombones* without the caricature characteristic of the American white writers who have dealt with the theme.

I think it may, moreover, be worthwhile to ask what is this mainstream of the contribution of the United States to world culture? It is not chauvinism but an objective determination of fact to remark that in the area of both popular and religious music, the American Negro is not a tributary; he is substantially the stream. With the alchemy of his particular talent, he transformed and practically pre-empted the field of American popular music through jazz and the blues. Out of his American passion, he created the tragic glory of the spirituals and his own inimitable gospel music, and he remains decisive in their development. And this he did not do through a preoccupation with the "respectable" or accepted musical forms about him, but in response to the interior demands of his being.

Thus far the United States as a nation—young, frontier, and materialistic—has made but a modest contribution to the world's cultural riches. The American Negro, with his aesthetic talent and with the deeper spiritual insight of his long and not yet ended ordeal, may well betray not only his future possibilities in the United States but, more importantly, his potential cultural and spiritual contribution to humanity by fixing in his mind a pattern of his role as a subordinate part of a greater whole, a whole which has traditionally denied him dignity and his full stature as a human being.

James Weldon Johnson wrote in *Along This Way* that the Negro may be ultimately merged in America, but that he had beforehand a distinct cultural contribution to make. Cedrec Dover, the Indian writer, at the Paris Congress three years ago, decried the fact that the drive toward integration in the United States seems to mean for many American Negroes a desire for obliteration and passive absorption by the majority. He remarked that a close and fruitful rapport between people can occur only where there is complete respect for the identity of the one by the other. It is this truth that Ralph Waldo Emerson, who keynoted a second independence from Britain, undoubtedly had in mind when he said in effect that a quality of the highest type of friendship was the ability to do without.

And to achieve this birth of freedom from the culture prison, let us finally consider more precisely whether the American Negro writer has an interest in looking to that phase of what the French African terms negritude, the African heritage. Is he cut off by 300 years of his American experience? Undoubtedly, he will never draw upon this experience in the manner or with the intensity of the writer on the African continent. But since the dominant American image of the Negro, which is held by Negro and white alike and which robs the Negro of his full stature, is due in large measure to the popular distorted impression of Africa and her peoples as a continent of barbarism, would it not be valuable, even imperative, to break through that culture prison and to deal with this poisonous current that feeds the American stream?

It is a necessary task, and in the historical light of the interaction of cultures, there is no reason why the African heritage may not be, for those who are so inclined, a fertile source of inspiration. For these it will be futile to admonish that our roots are American only, that our roots go back to the Virginia shore in 1619 and stop at the water's edge amid the branding and the cries and trancelike intonations such as those of Cassandra when carried by Agamemnon back to Greece: "What isle, what land is this?"

Perhaps, therefore, our concern with Africa should stop with 1619. But here in New York a German philosopher once said the connective most applicable to man is not "therefore," but "nonetheless." What was the direct line from Greece to Arabia? And yet through Arabian scholars such as Avicenna and Avarroes, a milennium removed, antiquity was recaptured and became the inspiration for the Renaissance of Western Europe. When Derain chanced upon a piece of African statuary in a street in France, his remoteness from the former continent did not prevent him, or Picasso and others of the cubists and the "fauves," from finding in that work an inspiration for an entirely new direction—a new dimension in Western art. A more immediate example: last year at the Schomburg collection in Harlem, Randy Weston, a jazz pianist and composer was doing research in African rhythms, which he has employed in the creations he has since played here at the Birdland and elsewhere. In literature, the poetry of Countee Cullen, Langston Hughes, Melvin Tolson, and Claude McKay has already, in varying degrees, occupied itself with the African past.

It is impossible to know beforehand to what extent the African heritage may be utilized by the American Negro writer or by any American writer for that matter. Experience, not a predetermined chart, will provide the answer. I do not feel that the Negro writer's identity as an American precludes him from a substantial participation in that rich heritage.

On the South Atlantic coastline of this country there is an expression that has survived slavery—the expression "gone to Guinea." When the old African woman was weary from her labor in the Carolina fields or from her chores about the house, when she was overcome by the troubles of the world, she would say that soon she would be "gone to Guinea," that is, she would die and go to heaven. Guinea *was* heaven. Guinea was the West Coast of Africa which remained but faintly, nostalgically in the memory of her shattered past. As part of the continuing effort of the American Negro to find his roots, to achieve his full stature not only as a member of American society but as a man, I think it may be fruitful to go back for a moment in our cultural reconnaissance—to go back to Guinea.

In conclusion, it should be pointed out again that there are two phases of this development among the African poets. We have just considered the preoccupation with the content of the African past. Here, the fact that the social, economic, and political organization of the American Negro is part of the American society is evident. It could not be otherwise. And although Carter Woodson, W. E. B. Du Bois, and others mounted a continuing attack upon the Robert S. Park school of thought that the Negro was completely bereft of his cultural past when he was transplanted to these shores, yet it appears undisputed that here there was no substantial African influence in the shaping of American institutions. This fact, however, as we have seen in the history of the interaction of cultures, is by no means decisive as to the value of the one in affording a source of inspiration and renewal for the other. The American Negro as a group will undoubtedly in the long run be pre-eminently concerned with the American scene. Yet Africa may well serve for many as a leaven, enriching in large measure the cultural loaf.

There is, finally, that aspect of negritude which, as we have pointed out, has not to do with an African content, but which is simply an affirmation of self, of that dwarfed self, denied realization because of the root of its identity. (And that is the meaning of the word "race." It comes from *raiz*, meaning "root.") It is clear that the American Negro, like the African, has an imposing interest in the development of his image of the universe, in the correction of the distorted image of himself in this society, and in an exploration and a fuller expression of his particular talents, whatever the subject matter with which he deals. It is true that, though historically oppressed and excluded from its privileges, we are part of the American whole and subject to its influences. The problem is one of emphasis within a continuing dialectic of forces. Both points of view have their reality. But we cannot resolve the argument by a kind of generous eclecticism. It is vital to assess the degree of emphasis and the particular emphasis appropriate to our cultural situation. That emphasis at present would most fruitfully be in the insistence upon our unique creative personality; and it should continue to be so until we have achieved our full identity, implicit in our culture without the necessity of affirmation, until we have purged the empoisoned mainstream, until the metamorphosis implicit in the lines of Césaire has taken place: "bird of their scorn, bird reborn, brother in the sun." This may be termed a kind of cultural treason. It is not. It may be termed, in a pejorative sense, romanticism. Again, it is not. But pleading in the alternative, if it be, it is our opportunity to make the most of it.

PART III

REAPPRAISAL OF THE BLACK CULTURAL EXPERIENCE IN AMERICA

HAROLD WRIGHT CRUSE

Harold Cruse is a literary critic and essayist who is presently Writer-in-Residence at the University of Michigan. He has gained national acclaim for his interpretative study *The Crisis of the Negro Intellectual*, published in 1967. Cruse was born in Virginia and later lived in New York. He has contributed to a variety of publications, including *Liberator*, *Negro Digest*, and *Temps Modernes*. He was also one of the participants in the Yale Symposium on Black Studies in 1969.

In his essay, "An Afro-American's Cultural Views," Cruse attempts to explain why the growing political activity of the black in the United States has not been accompanied by a comparable cultural movement. The interpretations expressed in this article are treated more fully in *The Crisis of the Negro Intellectual*.

FURTHER READING: Robert Chrisman. "The Crisis of Harold Cruse," *Black Scholar*, I, 1 (1969), pp. 77–84.

Harold Wright Cruse

From An Afro-American's Cultural Views

For Africans at home and abroad, the cultural situation of the American Negro might seem vague and incomprehensible amidst the general civil rights struggle in this country. For the simple reason that American Negroes are part of the colored peoples of the world, it is easy for one to make the error of assuming that we Negroes here in the United States have a cultural outlook in terms of race, nationality, history, and traditions similar in racial uniqueness to other colored nations the world over who are rising to national independence out of colonialism. When one speaks of a culture in the creative sense one thinks of art, literature, music, drama, dance, language, skills and crafts, architecture, etc., and when one thinks of the liberation of oppressed peoples one assumes a rebirth and a flowering of that people's native "culture" as a corollary of the rise to independence. Thus, in keeping with what is happening to colored peoples elsewhere one might expect that in the United States the increased activity on the part of Negroes to achieve full citizenship, equality, and civil rights under the law would be accompanied by an increase in quantity and quality of his "cultural" activities. Unfortunately, this is not the case. Why is this?

* * *

The American Negro cannot be understood culturally unless he is seen as a detached ethnic bloc of people of African descent reared for three hundred years in the unmotherly bosom of western civilization. With regards to the African motherland, the American Negro is not an African, not even remotely. Not only has three hundred years of time separated him culturally from Africa but, also, has several thousand miles of geographical distance cut him off from any

Source: Harold W. Cruse's article "An Afro-American's Cultural Views" published in No. 17 of the review *Présence africaine*, Paris (December 1957–January 1958), pp. 31–38. Reprinted by permission of the publisher.

kind of real communication with Africa. As a detached offshoot of African peoples he is isolated, cut off, and has been subjected to racial intermingling in the process. Today he is a racial mixture of African, Indian, and Caucasian, and writers like William E. B. Du Bois, the sociologist, claim that only a small percentage of American Negroes can be classified as pure "African." There are many American Negroes who condemn the use of the word "Negro" as being a synonym for inferiority, and we have a weekly newspaper which does not print the word "Negro" anywhere in its pages. It uses the word "colored" instead. Some Negroes prefer the hyphenation Afro-American to correspond not only to our actual historical origin, but to the social status of other national and ethnic groups such as the Irish-American, Jewish-American, Italian-American, etc. Such Negroes feel that Afro-American would lend more dignity to the meaning of our racial heritage and would also raise the American Negro as a racial minority to political and social equality with other American minorities, at least nominally. There are also Negroes who do not like the term Afro-American since they especially eschew any affinities with Africa either by color or culture. Clearly then, we American Negroes do not agree on what we actually are or on what we shall call ourselves.

However, without intending to deny the obvious, that is our African antecedents, we must keep in mind that three hundred years of rearing in the United States has separated us from Africa in ways more insurmountable, culturally speaking, than time gaps of centuries if the present attitudes of our Afro-American intellectuals and artists are any indication. It must be clearly understood that our racial and cultural experience as a group is distinctly American. The African languages, customs, religion, traditions, of our forbears were discouraged and eventually destroyed by the necessities of the slave system. This de-Africanization process actually began at the point of landing of slaves on American shores. There slaves were detribalized almost immediately, destroying any means of unity and communication. There began the process of westernization. We adopted the Caucasian's language—English, his religion, as many customs as conditions permitted, including the eight-toned musical scale brought from Europe to America. Most slaves who learned to read English learned it from the Holy Bible. Emancipation from chattel slavery brought on by the Civil War between the northern and southern states (1861–1865) marked the beginning of a long, bitter struggle on the part of Afro-Americans for political, social, and economic equality, objectives which are still far from being fully achieved. During slavery and for several decades after emancipation it was possible for one to say that Afro-Americans had a distinct culture although there is much contention on this claim by scholars and laymen. Nevertheless, Afro-Americans produced a distinct body of social art embodied in music, song, dance, folklore, poetry, formal literature, craftsmanship, mores, and even their own variant of Christian religious expression and experience. Much of this culture was of the "folk quality" and more sophisticated expressions of this culture developed along with our rise in social status after emancipation. We produced novelists, poets, journalists, historians, a few dramatists, painters, sculptors. In the music field we have been outstanding both in quantity and quality of musical creativity. American Negro jazz music and its concomitant dance patterns have given America its unique musical complexion and have influenced the western world. The American musical theater owes its character to American Negro music and dance creative genius so much so that today our music and dance has been fully incorporated into the broad quality of being "American." In the theater we have had notable successes of a certain kind due chiefly to our pioneering abilities in music, song, and dance but this must be accepted with certain serious reservations for reasons which will be considered further on in this article. It can be seen then, that despite our separation from the ways of Africa, the Afro-American produced a culture that is distinctly his own and for the most part, American in general milieu. It would be assumed then that because of our overall rise in social, economic, and political status our Afro-American cultural heritage would find higher, fuller, more creative, more profound, more classical, more influential, more universal expression for all its uniqueness in the western world. For we are unique in the sense that we are a rather large non-white racial bloc of a stature of internationally strategic importance in the west. Yet it must be said that what we should be achieving "culturally" as Afro-Americans is not being achieved and is not in the immediate offing.

* * *

There has been no cultural upsurge commensurate with our stepped up struggle for political and social equality. Hence it behooves Africans at home and abroad, when speaking of Afro-American "culture" in the United States, to first examine and understand the philosophy which Negro leaders have adopted and applied to our fight for full citizenship. Today our struggle for complete racial equality in all areas of American life is summed up in the rallying slogans of "racial integration" or "full integration." Racial Integration is the guiding outlook and philosophy of the National Association for the Advancement of Colored People, the Urban League, both leading American Negro pressure groups for civil rights. Racial Integration is the racial philosophy of certain individual leaders and race spokesmen such as Martin Luther King, Jr., and a long list of public figures. The implications of the philosophy of "Racial Integration" vis-à-vis the idea of a legitimate Afro-American racial culture in the United States is a subject which is not being publicly debated and classified. Yet it lingers under the surface of an active sea of racial and interracial events like a powerful unseen social tide; inexorably present despite the agitation and clamor above. Let us now explore some of these implications.

When one speaks of the Afro-American and "culture" one has to be certain what one means. This writer is a member of the National Association for the Advancement of Colored People (NAACP). On the back of my membership card there are listed six objectives having to do with educating Americans on Negro rights, wiping out lynching, securing the franchise, securing protective legislation against prejudice, etc. Item number five in this list of objectives reads: "To stimulate the cultural life of Negroes." This can mean many things to many people depending upon what certain people mean by "cultural life." Does it mean the stimulation of Afro-American cultural expression as a thing in itself? Or does it mean the stimulation of Negro activity in the broad avenues of general "American culture"? For one to say that it means simply the participation of Afro-Americans in all-embracing "culture" which is an amalgam of all the racial and national minorities in the United States including that of our prime human stock, the Anglo-American, is much easier said as an oversimplification of American realities than done, inasmuch as this idealistic amalgamation of races, and nationalities in the United States does not exist. The proposition "To stimulate the cultural life of Negroes" has posed a question which has not been answered. Africans at home and abroad to whom this is addressed can hardly expect a forthright answer from us Afro-Americans since we have not been able to answer it for ourselves. This inability to find an appropriate answer has caused us to lapse into a state of the most unbelievable intellectual confusion, immobility, and lassitude in matters of art, literature, and cultural creativity. We are in a severe cultural crisis!

*   *   *

The root of the Afro-American's problems in the cultural fields is a debilitating sickness whose diagnosis is Caucasian idolatry in the arts, abandonment of true identity, immature childlike mimicry of white aesthetics. Many Afro-Americans express this trend willingly, as a matter of choice, as a way of life based on class origins, skin color, and personal affinities. Many others are being asked or compelled to accept it as a sacrifice or a price for full racial equality or "full integration." In the theater one hears such talk as this: "I am an actor, not just a Negro actor" or "I am interested in theater, not just Negro theater" or "Negroes should be writers, not just Negro writers." This is the verbalization of the idea that to be a "Negro actor" or a "Negro writer" or to espouse a "Negro theater" as an institutional thing is self-proscribing and self-segregating. Whatever one might think of such views on art, the reality of the American cultural scene has proven these views to be self-defeating because most of this talk is heard during the long stretches of unemployment experienced by Afro-Americans who try to make a living and perfect their craft in the acting fields. Moreover, when work is available Negroes are not hired just as "actors" to play any kind of a role on Broadway, television, or in films. They are hired to portray Negro characterizations as Negroes in stories or plays usually written by whites. The dream of many Negro actors who wish to be hired to portray "any role" which actually means "white" roles remains merely a dream. As for Negro writers it is even more ridiculous for people to say "Negroes who write should be universal, not just Negro writers." Perhaps Negro writers should write "universally" but in actuality Negro writers produce little enough literature of quality about the life they know best (or should know). It remains a puzzle to this writer how Negroes can be expected to develop to be "universal" when they avoid the wealth of racial literary material "in their own backyard." In any event little appears from our writers either racial or otherwise.

* * *

The Afro-American writer, actor, artist, etc., has succumbed almost completely to middle-class values of art, living, and thinking. The Afro-American middle-class has real love for art, racial or otherwise. When Negro individuals enter the art fields such as the performing arts, art becomes in most cases a steppingstone to middle-class living which involves adopting the white standards in art in the fields in which they aspire, the better to cross the racial bridge. Hence, racially conscious writers, actors, directors, dancers, painters, etc., can look for no financial support from the Afro-American middle-class in furthering racial art in any form. These aspects—the class and economic factors of Afro-American culture—suggest an approach that has not been given serious study although the way has now been cleared by the appearance of E. Franklin Frazier's brilliant study of the Negro middle-class and its role in Negro life. It is hoped that this reevaluation of Negro culture will come in the very near future for the Afro-American needs at this time to regain a new grip and a reorientation on his identity. Many rank-and-file Negroes have recently remarked to this writer that the Negro is a "lost race," "that the white man has destroyed the Negro's ability to think for himself," "that he is free in body but enslaved in mind," "that he is not really making progress in spite of all the noise about civil rights," "that he has no philosophy of his own," "the Negro has no unity," etc. This is the outlook of countless ordinary Negroes but the racial integration philosophy has gripped the outlook of the Negro middle-class. It is a philosophy that is meant to further their own class aims and the aspirations of the masses only incidentally. Middle-class Negroes do not identify with the masses or the cultural needs of the masses and every rationalization is used by the middle-class to justify its views.

* * *

From all this it is clear that assimilation tendencies in the outlooks of Afro-American intellectuals, artists, writers, etc., have made our cultural problem a very complex one. It is for this reason I believe the Negro problem in the United States to be primarily a cultural question, yet it is just the cultural side of the question which is the most overlooked and neglected. On the cultural plane of our American existence we find keys to questions of identity, cultural values expressed in group institutional forms, standards for judgment in literature, art, music, dance, drama, poetry, and racial historiography. It seems to me that the Afro-American cannot take a firm grip on his own destiny in the United States until there comes a wholehearted effort on his part to essay a cultural rehabilitation and refurbishing of his entire racial outlook. This in no way implies that politics and economics are unimportant; it does mean that all things in life are relative. In the United States, the Afro-American can never dominate politics or economics. Being a racial minority, without an ownership class all that he has in economics to offer are labor and purchasing power, he is not a producer and his economic fortunes are tied to the rise and fall of American productive prosperity as a whole. In politics, our lack of economic controlling power renders our political bargaining power effective only during presidential elections when our votes are sought after numerically. However, smaller racial minorities in the United States wield infinitely greater political and economic power than we. Progress for the Afro-American then demands the strongest kind of racial unity and cooperative endeavor. But racial unity cannot be had in the face of the extreme racial and cultural diffidence towards our heritage which is evident in our racial outlook these days. It is for this reason that I believe our problem is fundamentally a cultural one. The entire question is broad and complicated and requires intensive study. What has been said here is purely one Afro-American's attitude to things seen and felt on the surface of our community life. The whole question involves separate treatment of the many different trends, institutions, and personalities in Negro cultural life, for example, the future of Negro music, the problem of the Negro novel, and the economic and class aspect of Negroes in art, the question of Paul Robeson as a major cultural figure, etc. It is hoped that an opportunity will be found to present some views on these different aspects sometime in the very near future.

MALCOLM X

Born Malcolm Little in Omaha, Nebraska, in 1925, Malcolm X rose rapidly to become one of the leading black spokesmen in this country. Until a short period before his assassination in 1965, he was an ardent advocate of black nationalism and a strong supporter of Islam as the meaningful and nonracist religion for blacks. He had become a convert to the Nation of Islam, founded by Elijah Muhammed, while he was serving a prison sentence for burglary. Upon his release from jail, he became Elijah Muhammed's right-hand man but broke with the Nation of Islam in 1964 and established his own Muslim Mosque, Inc. He also founded the Organization of Afro-American Unity, modeled on the Organization of African Unity, and designed to resolve the differences existing among American blacks and to unite them in a forceful organization.

Malcolm X's significance and popularity have increased since his death; his name is today familiar to most Americans, many of whom know him through his moving *Autobiography*. Yet Malcolm X was neither an original nor a profound mind; his ability lay in his juxtaposition of ideas that went to the heart of the race problem and in his expression of a new mood growing among blacks in the United States. His real strength was as a speaker, and, as most critics insist, his speeches are best heard, not read.

If he did not publicly consider at length black culture as such, his speeches indicate an interest in the African heritage and the commonalty of African and Afro-American problems.

FURTHER READING: *The Autobiography of Malcolm X.* New York: Grove Press, 1965.

Malcolm X

From *Malcolm X Speaks*

From his memorandum to the heads of state attending the Organization of African Unity conference at Cairo, July 17–21, 1964.

Since the 22 million of us were originally Africans, who are now in America not by choice but by a cruel accident in our history, we strongly believe that African problems are our problems and our problems are African problems.

Your Excellencies:

We also believe that as heads of the independent African states you are the shepherd of *all* African peoples everywhere, whether they are still at home on the mother continent or have been scattered abroad.

Some African leaders at this conference have implied that they have enough problems here on the mother continent without adding the Afro-American problem.

With all due respect to your esteemed positions, I must remind all of you that the good shepherd will leave ninety-nine sheep, who are safe at home, to go to the aid of the one who is lost and has fallen into the clutches of the imperialist wolf.

We, in America, are your long-lost brothers and sisters, and I am here only to remind you that our problems are your problems. As the African-Americans "awaken" today, we find ourselves in a strange land that has rejected us, and like the prodigal son, we are turning to our elder brothers for help. We pray our pleas will not fall upon deaf ears.

From a radio address, delivered February 14, 1965, in Detroit.

One of the things that made the Black Muslim movement grow was its emphasis upon things African. This was the secret to the

Source: Malcolm X, *Malcolm X Speaks*, pp. 73, 171–172, 212–213. Reprinted by permission of Pathfinder Press, Inc. Copyright © 1965 by Merit Publishers and Mrs. Betty Shabazz.

growth of the Black Muslim movement. African blood, African origin, African culture, African ties. And you'd be surprised—we discovered that deep within the subconscious of the black man in this country, he is still more African than he is American. He *thinks* that he's more American than African, because the man is jiving him, the man is brainwashing him every day. He's telling him, "You're an American, you're an American." Man, how could you think you're an American when you haven't ever had any kind of an American treat over here? You have never, never. Ten men can be sitting at a table eating, you know, dining, and I can come and sit down where they're dining. They're dining; I've got a plate in front of me, but nothing is on it. Because all of us are sitting at the same table, are all of us diners? I'm not a diner until you let me dine. Just being at the table with others who are dining doesn't make me a diner, and this is what you've got to get in your head here in this country.

From an interview, Young Socialist, March – April 1965.

I used to define black nationalism as the idea that the black man should control the economy of his community, the politics of his community, and so forth.

But, when I was in Africa in May, in Ghana, I was speaking with the Algerian ambassador who is extremely militant and is a revolutionary in the true sense of the word (and has his credentials as such for having carried on a successful revolution against oppression in his country). When I told him that my political, social, and economic philosophy was black nationalism, he asked me very frankly, well, where did that leave him? Because he was white. He was an African, but he was Algerian, and to all appearances he was a white man. And he said if I define my objective as the victory of black nationalism, where does that leave him? Where does that leave revolutionaries in Morocco, Egypt, Iraq, Mauritania? So he showed me where I was alienating people who were true revolutionaries, dedicated to overturning the system of exploitation that exists on this earth by any means necessary.

So I had to do a lot of thinking and reappraising of my definition of black nationalism. Can we sum up the solution to the problems confronting our people as black nationalism? And if you notice, I haven't been using the expression for several months. But I still would be hard pressed to give a specific definition of the over-all philosophy which I think is necessary for the liberation of black people in this country.

LEROI JONES

Today the most eminent black playwright in this country, Jones was born in Newark, New Jersey, in 1934. He studied at Rutgers and Howard universities and received a master's degree from Columbia University. Among his many activities, he founded the poetry magazine *Yugen* and was director of the controversial Black Arts Repertory Theatre in Harlem. Perhaps his best known plays are *The Dutchman* and *The Toilet*. He has written a novel entitled *The System of Dante's Hell* (1965), and an interpretative essay on music, *Blues People: Negro Music in White America* (1963). Now an outspoken advocate of black nationalism, Jones has followed the practice of many black radicals by adopting an Islamic name, Imamu Ameer Baraka.

The following essay selected from *Home* suggests the intensifying mood of blackness exhibited by Jones. Entitled "The Legacy of Malcolm X, and the Coming of the Black Nation," the article was written after the assassination of Malcolm X and is one of the most interesting interpretations of the work and achievements of that black militant leader.

FURTHER READING: D. Lorens. "Ameer (LeRoi Jones) Baraka, *Ebony*, August 1969, pp. 75–78.

LeRoi Jones

From The Legacy of Malcolm X, and the Coming of the Black Nation

Malcolm X's greatest contribution, other than to propose a path to internationalism and hence, the entrance of the American Black Man into a world-wide allegiance against the white man (in most recent times he proposed to do it using a certain kind of white liberal as a lever), was to preach Black Consciousness to the Black Man. As a minister for the Nation of Islam, Malcolm talked about a black consciousness that took its form from religion. In his last days he talked of another black consciousness that proposed politics as its moving energy.

But one very important aspect of Malcolm's earlier counsels was his explicit call for a National Consciousness among Black People. And this aspect of Malcolm's philosophy certainly did abide throughout his days. The feeling that somehow the Black Man was different, as being, as a being, and finally, in our own time, as judge. And Malcolm propounded these differences as life anecdote and religious (political) truth and made the consideration of Nationalist ideas significant and powerful in our day.

Another very important aspect of Malcolm's earlier (or the Honorable Elijah Muhammad's) philosophy was the whole concept of land and land-control as central to any talk of "freedom" or "independence." The Muslim tack of asking for land within the continental United States in which Black People could set up their own nation, was given a special appeal by Malcolm, even though the request was seen by most people outside the movement as "just talk" or the amusing howls of a gadfly.

But the whole importance of this insistence on land is just now

Source: From *Home: Social Essays* by LeRoi Jones, pp. 241–244, 247–248. Reprinted by permission of William Morrow and Company, Inc., and The Sterling Lord Agency. Copyright © 1965, 1966, 1968 by LeRoi Jones.

beginning to be understood. Malcolm said many times that when you speak about revolution you're talking about land—changing the ownership or usership of some specific land which you think is yours. But any talk of Nationalism also must take this concept of land and its primary importance into consideration because, finally, any Nationalism which is not intent on restoring or securing autonomous space for a people, i.e., a nation, is at the very least shortsighted.

Elijah Muhammad has said, "We want our people in America, whose parents or grandparents were descendants from slaves, to be allowed to establish a separate state or territory of their own—either on this continent or elsewhere. We believe that our former slavemasters are obligated to provide such land and that the area must be fertile and minerally rich." And the Black Muslims seem separate from most Black People because the Muslims have a national consciousness based on their aspirations for land. Most of the Nationalist movements in this country advocate that that land is in Africa, and Black People should return there, or they propose nothing about land at all. It is impossible to be a Nationalist without talking about land. Otherwise, your Nationalism is a misnamed kind of "difficult" opposition to what the white man has done, rather than the advocation of another people becoming the rulers of themselves, and sooner or later the rest of the world.

The Muslims moved from the Back-to-Africa concept of Marcus Garvey (the first large movement by Black People back to a National Consciousness, which was, finally, only viable when the Black Man focused on Africa as literally "back home") to the concept of a Black National Consciousness existing in this land the Black captives had begun to identify as home. (Even in Garvey's time, there was not a very large percentage of Black People who really wanted to leave. Certainly, the newly emerging Black bourgeoisie would have nothing to do with "returning" to Africa. They were already created in the image of white people, as they still are, and wanted nothing to do with Black.

What the Muslims wanted was a profound change. The National Consciousness focused on actual (nonabstract) land, identifying a people, in a land where they lived. Garvey wanted to go back to Jordan. A real one. The Nation of Islam wanted Jordan closer. Before these two thrusts, the Black Man in America, as he was Christianized, believed Jordan was in the sky, like pie, and absolutely supernatural.

Malcolm, then, wanted to give the National Consciousness its political embodiment, and send it out to influence the newly forming third world, in which this consciousness was to be included. The concept of Blackness, the concept of the National Consciousness, the proposal of a political (and diplomatic) form for this aggregate of Black spirit, these are the things given to us by Garvey, through Elijah Muhammad and finally given motion into still another area of Black response by Malcolm X.

Malcolm's legacy to Black People is what he moved toward, as the accretion of his own spiritual learning and the movement of Black People in general, through the natural hope, a rise to social understanding within the new context of the white nation and its decline under hypocrisy and natural "oppositeness" which has pushed all of us toward "new" ideas. We are all the products of national spirit and world view. We are drawn by the vibrations of the entire nation. If there were no bourgeois Negroes, none of us would be drawn to that image. They, bourgeois Negroes, were shaped through the purposive actions of a national attitude, and finally, by the demands of a particular culture.

At which point we must consider what cultural attitudes are, what culture is, and what National Consciousness has to do with these, i.e., if we want to understand what Malcolm X was pointing toward, and why the Black Man now must move in that direction since the world will not let him move any other way. The Black Man is possessed by the energies of historic necessity and the bursting into flower of a National Cultural Consciousness, and with that, into a living future, the shouldering to power of Black culture and, finally, Black Men . . . and then, Black ideals, which are different descriptions of a God. A righteous sanctity, out of which worlds are built.

* * *

Western Culture (the way white people live and think) is passing. If the Black Man cannot identify himself as separate, and understand what this means, he will perish along with Western Culture and the white man.

What a culture produces, is, and refers to, is an image—a picture of a process, since it is a form of a process: movement seen. The changing of images, of references, is the Black Man's way back to the racial integrity of the captured African, which is where we must take ourselves, in feeling, to be truly the warriors we propose to be. To form an absolutely rational attitude toward West man, and West thought. Which is what is needed. To see the white man as separate and as enemy. To make a fight according to the absolute realities of the world as it is.

Good-Bad, Beautiful-Ugly, are all formed as the result of image. The mores, customs, of a place are the result of experience, and a common reference for defining it—common images. The three white men in the film *Gunga Din* who kill off hundreds of Indians, Greek hero-style, are part of an image of white men. The various black porters, gigglers, ghostchumps, and punkish Indians, etc., that inhabit the public image the white man has fashioned to characterize Black Men are references by Black Men to the identity of Black Men in the West, since that's what is run on them each day by white magic, i.e., television, movies, radio, etc.—the Mass Media (the *Daily News* does it with flicks and adjectives).

The song title "A White Man's Heaven Is a Black Man's Hell" describes how complete an image reversal is necessary in the West. Because for many Black People, the white man has succeeded in making this hell seem like heaven. But Black youth are much better off in this regard than their parents. They are the ones who need the least image reversal.

The Black artist, in this context, is desperately needed to change the images his people identify with, by asserting Black feeling, Black mind, Black judgment. The Black intellectual, in this same context, is needed to change the interpretation of facts toward the Black Man's best interests, instead of merely tagging along reciting white judgments of the world.

Art, Religion, and Politics are impressive vectors of a culture. Art describes a culture. Black artists must have an image of what the Black sensibility is in this land. Religion elevates a culture. The Black Man must aspire to Blackness. God is man idealized. The Black Man must idealize himself as Black. And idealize and aspire to that. Politics gives a social order to the culture, i.e., makes relationships within the culture definable for the functioning organism. The Black Man must seek a Black politics, an ordering of the world that is beneficial to his culture, to his interiorization and judgment of the world. This is strength. And we are hordes.

PART IV

RECENT CRITICISMS AND NEW DIRECTIONS

FRANTZ FANON

Frantz Fanon is the ideologue as Che Guevera is the folk-hero of adherents to contemporary political radicalism the world over. A man whose meteoric life ended in an early and tragic death from cancer in 1961, he involved himself in and wrote of revolutionary activity. Born in Martinique in 1925, he was educated in Paris where he received his medical degree and also underwent a psychic experience of cultural uprootedness, much as his fellow countryman, Aimé Césaire, had done before him. Out of this experience he wrote *Black Skins, White Masks*, which is one of the most perceptive treatments of white racism and its psychological effects that has been written. A study that shows Fanon's wide and sensitive reading, as well as the deep probing of his mind, it exhibits a prose style that at times borders on the lyrical.

Probably the most original of Fanon's literary contributions, *Black Skins, White Masks* does not, however, compare with *The Wretched of the Earth* in influence or popularity. This later volume, first published in 1961, emerged from the experiences Fanon had had as a doctor serving with the National Liberation Front during the Algerian war for independence. As he perceived that struggle, violence was a necessary and therapeutic response to colonialism. "Colonialism . . . is violence in its natural state, and it will yield only when confronted with greater violence." For the colonized, the violent struggle for independence was a means to reach social-psychological catharsis, for in redeeming his country he was redeeming himself, acquiring that personality denied him by the colonizer.

While Fanon's analysis derived directly from the Algerian situation, both he and his ideological followers extended the argument to Third World dimensions. The cover of one paperback version of the book reads: "The Handbook for the Black Revolution that is changing the shape of the world."

Fanon appreciated the significance of culture in fostering and maintaining newly emerging states and societies. However, he argued against the notion of a common black culture having universal application and relevancy. It was his belief that every culture was a national culture, meeting the needs and reflecting the aspirations of that particular community.

FURTHER READING: David Caute, *Frantz Fanon*. New York: The Viking Press, Inc., 1970.

Frantz Fanon

From *The Wretched of the Earth*

I am ready to concede that on the plane of factual being the past existence of an Aztec civilisation does not change anything very much in the diet of the Mexican peasant of today. I admit that all the proofs of a wonderful Songhai civilisation will not change the fact that today the Songhais are under-fed and illiterate, thrown between sky and water with empty heads and empty eyes. But it has been remarked several times that this passionate search for a national culture which existed before the colonial era finds its legitimate reason in the anxiety shared by native intellectuals to shrink away from that Western culture in which they all risk being swamped. Because they realise they are in danger of losing their lives and thus becoming lost to their people, these men, hot-headed and with anger in their hearts, relentlessly determine to renew contact once more with the oldest and most precolonial springs of life of their people.

Let us go further. Perhaps this passionate research and this anger are kept up or at least directed by the secret hope of discovering beyond the misery of today, beyond self-contempt, resignation, and abjuration, some very beautiful and splendid era whose existence rehabilitates us both in regard to ourselves and in regard to others. I have said that I have decided to go further. Perhaps unconsciously, the native intellectuals, since they could not stand wonder-struck before the history of today's barbarity, decided to go back further and to delve deeper down; and, let us make no mistake, it was with the greatest delight that they discovered that there was nothing to be ashamed of in the past, but rather dignity, glory, and solemnity. The claim to a national culture in the past does not only rehabilitate that nation and serve as a justification for the hope of a future national culture. In

---

Source: Frantz Fanon, *The Wretched of the Earth*, pp. 169–172, 173–176, 187–188. Translated from the French by Constance Farrington. Reprinted by permission of Grove Press, Inc. Copyright © 1963 by Présence Africaine.

the sphere of psycho-affective equilibrium it is responsible for an important change in the native. Perhaps we have not sufficiently demonstrated that colonialism is not simply content to impose its rule upon the present and the future of a dominated country. Colonialism is not satisfied merely with holding a people in its grip and emptying the native's brain of all form and content. By a kind of perverted logic, it turns to the past of the oppressed people, and distorts, disfigures, and destroys it. This work of devaluing pre-colonial history takes on a dialectical significance today.

When we consider the efforts made to carry out the cultural estrangement so characteristic of the colonial epoch, we realise that nothing has been left to chance and that the total result looked for by colonial domination was indeed to convince the natives that colonialism came to lighten their darkness. The effect consciously sought by colonialism was to drive into the natives' heads the idea that if the settlers were to leave, they would at once fall back into barbarism, degradation, and bestiality.

On the unconscious plane, colonialism therefore did not seek to be considered by the native as a gentle, loving mother who protects her child from a hostile environment, but rather as a mother who unceasingly restrains her fundamentally perverse offspring from managing to commit suicide and from giving free rein to its evil instincts. The colonial mother protects her child from itself, from its ego, and from its physiology, its biology, and its own unhappiness which is its very essence.

In such a situation the claims of the native intellectual are no luxury but a necessity in any coherent programme. The native intellectual who takes up arms to defend his nation's legitimacy and who wants to bring proofs to bear out that legitimacy, who is willing to strip himself naked to study the history of his body, is obliged to dissect the heart of his people.

Such an examination is not specifically national. The native intellectual who decides to give battle to colonial lies fights on the field of the whole continent. The past is given back its value. Culture, extracted from the past to be displayed in all its splendour, is not necessarily that of his own country. Colonialism, which has not bothered to put too fine a point on its efforts, has never ceased to maintain that the Negro is a savage; and for the colonist, the Negro was neither an Angolan nor a Nigerian, for he simply spoke of "the Negro." For colonialism, this vast continent was the haunt of savages, a country riddled with superstitions and fanaticism, destined for contempt, weighed down by the curse of God, a country of cannibals—in short, the Negro's country. Colonialism's condemnation is continental in its scope. The contention by colonialism that the darkest night of humanity lay over pre-colonial history concerns the whole of the African continent. The efforts of the native to rehabilitate himself and to escape from the claws of colonialism are logically inscribed from the same point of view as that of colonialism. The native intellectual who has gone far beyond the domains of Western culture and who has got it into his head to proclaim the existence of another culture never does so in the name of Angola or of Dahomey. The culture which is affirmed is African culture. The Negro, never so much a Negro as since he has been dominated by the whites, when he decides to prove that he has a culture and to behave like a cultured person, comes to realize that history points out a well-defined path to him: he must demonstrate that a Negro culture exists.

And it is only too true that those who are most responsible for this racialisation of thought, or at least for the first movement towards that thought, are and remain those Europeans who have never ceased to set up white culture to fill the gap left by the absence of other cultures. Colonialism did not dream of wasting its time in denying the existence of one national culture after another. Therefore the reply of the colonised peoples will be straight away continental in its breadth. In Africa, the native literature of the last twenty years is not a national literature but a Negro literature. The concept of Negro-ism, for example, was the emotional if not the logical antithesis of that insult which the white man flung at humanity. This rush of Negro-ism against the white man's contempt showed itself in certain spheres to be the one idea capable of lifting interdictions and anathemas. Because the New Guinean or Kenyan intellectuals found themselves above all up against a general ostracism and delivered to the combined contempt of their overlords, their reaction was to sing praises in admiration of each other. The unconditional affirmation of African culture has succeeded the unconditional affirmation of European culture. On the whole, the poets of Negro-ism oppose the idea of an old Europe to a young Africa, tiresome reasoning to lyricism, oppressive logic to high-stepping nature, and on one side stiffness, ceremony, etiquette, and scepticism, while on the other frankness, liveliness, liberty and—why not?—luxuriance: but also irresponsibility.

The poets of Negro-ism will not stop at the limits of the continent. From America, black voices will take up the hymn with fuller unison. The "black world" will see the light and Busia from Ghana, Birago Diop from Senegal, Hampate Ba from the Soudan and Saint-Clair

Drake from Chicago will not hesitate to assert the existence of common ties and a motive power that is identical.

*   *   *

This historical necessity in which the men of African culture find themselves to racialise their claims and to speak more of African culture than of national culture will tend to lead them up a blind alley. Let us take for example the case of the African Cultural Society. This society had been created by African intellectuals who wished to get to know each other and to compare their experiences and the results of their respective research work. The aim of this society was therefore to affirm the existence of an African culture, to evaluate this culture on the plane of distinct nations and to reveal the internal motive forces of each of their national cultures. But at the same time this society fulfilled another need: the need to exist side by side with the European Cultural Society, which threatened to transform itself into a Universal Cultural Society. There was therefore at the bottom of this decision the anxiety to be present at the universal trysting place fully armed, with a culture springing from the very heart of the African continent. Now, this Society will very quickly show its inability to shoulder these different tasks, and will limit itself to exhibitionist demonstrations, while the habitual behaviour of the members of this Society will be confined to showing Europeans that such a thing as African culture exists, and opposing their ideas to those of ostentatious and narcissistic Europeans. We have shown that such an attitude is normal and draws its legitimacy from the lies propagated by men of Western culture. But the degradation of the aims of this Society will become more marked with the elaboration of the concept of Negro-ism. The African Society will become the cultural society of the black world and will come to include the Negro dispersion, that is to say the tens of thousands of black people spread over the American continents.

The Negroes who live in the United States and in Central or Latin America in fact experience the need to attach themselves to a cultural matrix. Their problem is not fundamentally different from that of the Africans. The whites of America did not mete out to them any different treatment from that of the whites that ruled over the Africans. We have seen that the whites were used to putting all Negroes in the same bag. During the first congress of the African Cultural Society which was held in Paris in 1956, the American Negroes of their own accord considered their problems from the same standpoint as those of their African brothers. Cultured Africans, speaking of African civilisations, decreed that there should be a reasonable status within the state for those who had formerly been slaves. But little by little the American Negroes realised that the essential problems confronting them were not the same as those that confronted the African Negroes. The Negroes of Chicago only resemble the Nigerians or the Tanganyikans in so far as they were all defined in relation to the whites. But once the first comparisons had been made and subjective feelings were assuaged, the American Negroes realised that the objective problems were fundamentally heterogeneous. The test cases of civil liberty whereby both whites and blacks in America try to drive back racial discrimination have very little in common in their principles and objectives with the heroic fight of the Angolan people against the detestable Portuguese colonialism. Thus, during the second congress of the African Cultural Society the American Negroes decided to create an American society for people of black cultures.

Negro-ism therefore finds its first limitation in the phenomena which take account of the formation of the historical character of men. Negro and African-Negro culture broke up into different entities because the men who wished to incarnate these cultures realised that every culture is first and foremost national, and that the problems which kept Richard Wright or Langston Hughes on the alert were fundamentally different from those which might confront Léopold Senghor or Jomo Kenyatta. In the same way certain Arab states, though they had chanted the marvellous hymn of Arab renaissance, had nevertheless to realise that their geographical position and the economic ties of their region were stronger even than the past that they wished to revive. Thus we find today the Arab states organically linked once more with societies which are Mediterranean in their culture. The fact is that these states are submitted to modern pressure and to new channels of trade while the network of trade relations which was dominant during the great period of Arab history has disappeared. But above all there is the fact that the political regimes of certain Arab states are so different, and so far away from each other in their conceptions that even a cultural meeting between these states is meaningless.

Thus we see that the cultural problem as it sometimes exists in colonised countries runs the risk of giving rise to serious ambiguities. The lack of culture of the Negroes, as proclaimed by colonialism, and the inherent barbarity of the Arabs ought logically to lead to the exaltation of cultural manifestations which are not simply national but continental, and extremely racial. In Africa, the movement of men of culture is a movement towards the Negro-African culture or the Arab-

Moslem culture. It is not specifically towards a national culture. Culture is becoming more and more cut off from the events of today. It finds its refuge beside a hearth that glows with passionate emotion, and from there makes its way by realistic paths which are the only means by which it may be made fruitful, homogeneous, and consistent.

If the action of the native intellectual is limited historically, there remains nevertheless the fact that it contributes greatly to upholding and justifying the action of politicians. It is true that the attitude of the native intellectual sometimes takes on the aspect of a cult or of a religion. But if we really wish to analyse this attitude correctly we will come to see that it is symptomatic of the intellectual's realisation of the danger that he is running in cutting his last moorings and of breaking adrift from his people. This stated belief in a national culture is in fact an ardent, despairing turning towards anything that will afford him secure anchorage. In order to ensure his salvation and to escape from the supremacy of the white man's culture the native feels the need to turn backwards towards his unknown roots and to lose himself at whatever cost in his own barbarous people. Because he feels he is becoming estranged, that is to say because he feels that he is the living haunt of contradictions which run the risk of becoming insurmountable, the native tears himself away from the swamp that may suck him down and accepts everything, decides to take all for granted and confirms everything even though he may lose body and soul. The native finds that he is expected to answer for everything, and to all comers. He not only turns himself into the defender of his people's past; he is willing to be counted as one of them, and henceforward he is even capable of laughing at his past cowardice.

* * *

The colonised man who writes for his people ought to use the past with the intention of opening the future as an invitation to action and a basis for hope. But to ensure that hope and to give it form, he must take part in action and throw himself body and soul into the national struggle. You may speak about everything under the sun; but when you decide to speak of that unique thing in man's life that is represented by the fact of opening up new horizons, by bringing light to your own country and by raising yourself and your people to their feet, then you must collaborate on the physical plane.

The responsibility of the native man of culture is not a responsibility vis-à-vis his national culture, but a global responsibility with regard to the totality of the nation, whose culture merely, after all, represents one aspect of that nation. The cultured native should not concern himself with choosing the level on which he wishes to fight or the sector where he decides to give battle for his nation. To fight for national culture means in the first place to fight for the liberation of the nation, that material key-stone which makes the building of a culture possible. There is no other fight for culture which can develop apart from the popular struggle. To take an example: all those men and women who are fighting with their bare hands against French colonialism in Algeria are not by any means strangers to the national culture of Algeria. The national Algerian culture is taking on form and content as the battles are being fought out, in prisons, under the guillotine, and in every French outpost which is captured or destroyed.

We must not therefore be content with delving into the past of a people in order to find coherent elements which will counteract colonialism's attempts to falsify and harm. We must work and fight with the same rhythm as the people to construct the future and to prepare the ground where vigorous shoots are already springing up. A national culture is not a folklore, nor an abstract populism that believes it can discover the people's true nature. It is not made up of the inert dregs of gratuitous actions, that is to say actions which are less and less attached to the ever-present reality of the people. A national culture is the whole body of efforts made by a people in the sphere of thought to describe, justify, and praise the action through which that people has created itself and keeps itself in existence. A national culture in under-developed countries should therefore take its place at the very heart of the struggle for freedom which these countries are carrying on. Men of African cultures who are still fighting in the name of African-Negro culture and who have called many congresses in the name of the unity of that culture should today realise that all their efforts amount to is to make comparisons between coins and sarcophagi.

EZEKIEL MPHAHLELE

Mphahlele was born in South Africa in 1919. After secondary education in Johannesburg, he received a teacher's certificate from Adam's College in Natal. He then taught English and Afrikaans in a Johannesburg high school, until governmental educational policies forced him from his job. He emigrated to Nigeria in 1957, where he taught at Ibadan, and then later worked as director of the African program of the Congress for Cultural Freedom in Paris. He has taught at Denver University and now is connected with University College in Nairobi. His autobiography, *Down Second Street*, was published in 1959, and his best-known work of criticism, *African Image*, was published in 1962.

Mphahlele has been a strong and frequent critic of negritude. His "Reply" was to a paper entitled "Negritude and Its Enemies," presented by W. Jeanpierre to the seminar on "African Literature and the University Curriculum" held at the University of Dakar in March 1963. Jeanpierre, an American black writer supporting the negritude thesis, said in comments directed to Mphahlele: "We totally reject those African writers who in the name of artistic integrity or because they declare themselves as being part of two different worlds attack and treat negritude with scorn."

FURTHER READING: Gerald Moore. *Seven African Writers*. New York: Oxford, University Press, Inc., 1967.

Ezekiel Mphahlele

A Reply

Yesterday I was personally attacked by someone because of my views against negritude. He charged me, in effect, with hindering or frustrating the protest literature of negritude, its mission. If I had not exiled myself from South Africa five years ago, after having lived for thirty-seven years in the South African nightmare, I should either have shrivelled up in my bitterness, or have been imprisoned for treason. My books have been banned in South Africa under a law that forbids the circulation of literature that is regarded as "objectionable, undesirable, or obscene." So you see what things I have been called in my life; my body itches from the number of labels that have been stuck on me! As for what I really am, and my place in the African revolution, I shall let my writings speak for me.

We in South Africa have for the last 300 years of oppression been engaged in a bloody struggle against white supremacy—to assert our *human* and not African dignity. This latter we have always taken for granted. During these three centuries, we the Africans have been creating an urban culture out of the very condition of insecurity, exile, and agony. We have done this by integrating Africa and the West. Listen to our music, see our dancing, and read our literature both in the indigenous and English languages. The bits of what the white ruling class calls "Bantu culture" that we are being told to "return to" are being used by that class to oppress us, to justify the Transkei and other Bantustans. And yet there still survive the toughest elements of African humanism which keep us together and supply the moral force which we need in a life that rejects us.

Source: Gerald Moore, ed., *African Literature and the Universities* (Ibadan: Ibadan University Press, 1965), pp. 22–26. Reprinted by permission of the publisher.

If you notice the two segregated sections of a town like Brazzaville, Congo, you cannot fail to see the sterile and purposeless life of the whites in their self-imposed ghetto as distinct from the vibrant and vigourous life of the black community. The blacks have reconciled the Western and African in them, while the whites refuse to surrender to their influence. This is symbolic of the South African situation. The only cultural vitality there is to be seen among the Africans: they have not been *uplifted* by a Western culture but rather they have reconciled the two in themselves. This is the sense in which I feel superior to the white man who refuses to be liberated by me as an African. So, anyone who imagines that we in South Africa are just helpless, groveling, and down-trodden creatures of two worlds who have been waiting for the "messiah" of negritude, does not know a thing about what is going on in our country. My detractor, as an American Negro who would like to teach us how to feel African, cites the entry of James Meredith into the University as symbolic of the triumph of the Negro's negritude in Mississippi. Are we really to believe that the U.S. Federal Army went to Mississippi to make it possible for Meredith to sing the blues or gospel songs? Surely his entry is to be seen as part of the Negro's campaign to be integrated socially and politically in the American population; to assert his human dignity. Of course, I am quite aware of certain—luckily there are few—non-African blacks and whites who came crawling on their bellies into this Continent as it were, prepared to be messengers or lackeys of some of us, prepared to eat the dust under our feet in self-abasement, in an attempt to identify with Africa. Such people are prompted to do this out of a guilt complex whereby they seek to bear the sins of past colonisers who, they imagine, we associate them with. Elsewhere I have warned against this ugly self-abasement because it prevents the "patient" from criticizing adversely anything the African says or writes, ripe, raw, and rotten. I fully agree with James Baldwin when he says in a brilliant and most moving essay in a recent issue of *The New Yorker* (17 November 1962), that the Negro must solve his problem inside America, not by a romantic identification with Africa. I appreciate also his remark that the Negro refuses to be integrated "into a burning house," i.e. the American social and political life that is sadly misguided, in which whites do not believe in death. And yet he also says that white and black in the U.S. need each other badly, that the white American needs to be liberated from himself but can only do this when he has liberated the Negro. After this, integration must come. Although he appreciates the Black Muslims, he foresees that one day he may have to fight them because they are such a menace.

Now to negritude itself. Who is so stupid as to deny the historical fact of negritude as both a protest and a positive assertion of African cultural values? All this is valid. What I do not accept is the way in which too much of the poetry inspired by it romanticizes Africa—as a symbol of innocence, purity, and artless primitiveness. I feel insulted when some people imply that Africa is not also a violent continent. I am a violent person, and proud of it because it is often a healthy human state of mind; someday I'm going to plunder, rape, set things on fire; I'm going to cut someone's throat; I'm going to subvert a government; I'm going to organize a *coup d'état;* yes, I'm going to oppress my own people; I'm going to hunt down the rich fat black men who bully the small, weak black men and destroy them; I'm going to become a capitalist, and woe to all who cross my path or who want to be my servants or chauffeurs and so on; I'm going to lead a breakway church—there is money in it; I'm going to attack the black bourgeoisie while I cultivate a garden, rear dogs and parrots; listen to jazz and classics, read "culture" and so on. Yes, I'm also going to organize a strike. Don't you know that sometimes I kill to the rhythm of drums and cut the sinews of a baby to cure it of paralysis? . . . This is only a dramatisation of what Africa can do and is doing. The image of Africa consists of all these and others. And negritude poetry pretends that they do not constitute the image and leaves them out. So we are told only half—often even a falsified half—of the story of Africa. Sheer romanticism that fails to see the large landscape of the personality of the African makes bad poetry. The omission of these elements of a continent in turmoil reflects a defensive poetic vision. The greatest poetry of Léopold Sédar Senghor is that which portrays in himself the meeting point of Europe and Africa. This is the most realistic and honest and meaningful symbol of Africa, an ambivalent continent searching for equilibrium. This synthesis of Europe and Africa does not necessarily reject the negro-ness of the African.

What have we to say about "benevolent dictatorship"; chauvinists, peasants who find that they have to change a way of life they have cherished for centuries and have to live in the twentieth century. Let me italicize again: an image of Africa that glosses over or dismisses these things is not a faithfully conceived one; it restricts our emotional and intellectual response. An image of Africa that only glorifies our ancestors and celebrates our "purity" and "innocence" is an image of a continent lying in state. When I asked at the Accra Congress of Africanists last December how long our poets are going to continue to bleat like goats in the act of giving birth, I was suggesting that Ghanaian poets should start looking inward, into themselves. Now I am being accused of encouraging "artistic purity" by asking writers to cease protesting against a colonial boss that has left their country. What is "artistic purity"? Am I being asked to lay the ghost of *l'art pour l'art*? Surely meaningful art has social significance or relevance and this very fact implies social criticism—protest in the broadest sense of the word. Gorky, Dostoevsky, Tolstoy, Dickens, and so on did this, but they were no less Russian or English; certainly they were much more committed than negritude poets. They took in the whole man. Camara Laye's *Le Regard du Roi*, Ferdinand Oyono's *Le Vieux Nègre et la Médaille* and Mongo Beti's *Le Pauvre Christ de Bomba* are not bullied by negritude. They are concerned in portraying the black-white encounter, and they do this, notwithstanding, with a devastating poetic sense of irony unmatched by any that one sees in the English novel by Africans (there are some fascinating works in the three main Bantu languages in South Africa which are of the same standard). I am suggesting here that we as writers need to be emancipated from ourselves. Negritude, while a valuable slogan politically, can, because its apostles have set it up as a principle of art, amount to self-enslavement—*autocolonisation*, to quote a French writer speaking of African politics and economics. We should not allow ourselves to be bullied at gun-point into producing literature that is supposed to contain a negritude theme and style. For now we are told, also, that there is *un style negro-africain*, and that therefore we have to sloganize and write to a march. We are told that negritude is less a matter of theme than style. We must strive to visualize the whole man, not merely the things that are meant to flatter the Negro's ego. Let it not be forgotten, too, that negritude has an overlap of 19th-century European protest against machines and canons. In the place of the cuckoo, the nightingale, the daffodil, Africa has been dragged to the altar of Europe. Negritude men should not pretend that this is an entirely African concept.

Several of us, as a result of the physical and mental agony we have been going through in South Africa, have rejected Christianity or any other religion as a cure for human ills. But if I wrote a poem or novel expressly to preach against religion without seeing the irony of the good and the bad done in the name of religion; if I omitted the irony of Christians and educated Africans who still revere ancestral spirits, and several other ironies and paradoxes, then it would not be a lasting work of art. I think that a writer who is too sure about his rejection of the use of a god can be as overbearing as the one who is too sure of his need for the existence of a god, like Browning. I say, then, that negritude can go on as a socio-political slogan, but that it has no right to set itself up as a standard of literary performance; there I refuse to go along. I refuse to be put in a Negro file—for sociologists to come and examine me. Art unifies even while it distinguishes men; and I regard it as an insult to the African for anyone to suggest that because we write independently on different themes in divers modes and styles all over Africa, therefore we are ripe victims of balkanization. But then I speak as a simple practising writer, not as a politician or a philosopher, or a non-African Africanist who is looking for categories and theories for a doctorate thesis. I refuse to be put in a dossier. And yet I am no less committed to the African revolution, to the South African freedom fight. The South African, East African, and English-speaking West African do not worry over negritude because they have never lost the essence of their negro-ness. Again, let negritude make the theme of literature if people want to use it. But we must remember that literature springs from an individual's experience, and in its effort to take in the whole man, it also tries to see far ahead, to project a prophetic vision, such as the writer is capable of, based on contemporary experience. It must at least set in motion vibrations in us that will continue even after we have read it, prompting us to continue inquiring into its meaning. If African culture is worth anything at all, it should not require myths to prop it up. These thoughts are not new at all. I have come to them after physical and mental agony. And it is, of course, not my monopoly either. It is the price Africa had to pay. And if you thought that the end of colonialism was the end of the agony, then it is time to wake up.

The fear that university teachers who distrust negritude or reject it as a principle of art may exclude from the syllabus literature inspired by this school, does not do justice to them. And the suggestion that they have a grave responsibility when they decide which African authors have to be taught is insulting to their intelligence. Why should they feel more responsible than they have been in the teaching of French? Is African writing in French not French literature? I am sure university teachers can be trusted to distinguish literature from a sociological or anthropological document that masquerades as literature! They can examine actual texts, can't they? Why should *la littérature engagée* be so spoiled as to want to be judged by different standards from those that have been tested by tradition?

We acknowledge that negritude as a socio-political concept defines the mind of the assimilated African in French-speaking territories. The British never set out to assimilate their colonial subjects. They hate to see people come out of their culture to emulate them (the British). They like the exotic African, not the one who tries to speak, walk, and eat like them. They love Africans in museum cases, so they left much of African culture intact. But literature and art are too big for negritude, and it had better be left as a historical phase.

STANISLAS ADOTEVI

Adotevi, who is Commissioner General for Culture and Youth in the African state of Dahomey, presented "The Strategy of Culture" at the Pan-African Cultural Festival, held in Algiers in the summer of 1969. The essay was not only one of the most striking offered but also it was one of the most enthusiastically received.

The Festival was the first major one held since the International Festival of Negro Arts met in Dakar in 1966, and the final celebration of negritude. The Algiers conference was a broader cultural undertaking and something of a rejoinder to negritude. President Touré of Guinea led the criticism when he argued that African leadership should never allow itself to be led, among other things, by the "false concepts of negritude."

In the paper delivered at Algiers, Adotevi provided one of the most forceful criticisms of negritude as a meaningful ideology for contemporary Africa.

FURTHER READING: Nathan Hare. "Report on the Pan-African Cultural Festival," *Black Scholar*, I, 1 (1969), pp. 2–10.

Stanislas Adotevi

From The Strategy of Culture

We need a philosophy, because in order to liberate the boundless activity which is culture and live fully what Marx called the generic essence of man, every African must free himself from spells and ghosts, or in other words from under-development, which is the immediate expression or consequence of neo-colonization.

Under-development, as we now know, is the presence of absence in the present, the mythical character in a debased drama named neo-colonization. It is neo-colonization which fills the stage of today's events with both actors and scenery, which robs the wakeful state of its certainty. It is a mysterious force whence issue the emanations of eternal exploitation, the matrix from which fetishes are endlessly turned out. It is this which makes and unmakes governments. Every African brought into its service, like Caliban by Prospero's wand, is working only to accomplish its desires.

Therefore, since in Africa there is no reality except through this savage fiction, the extraordinary resilience of which Césaire spoke and which all of us wish for can only come about through the projection over the whole of Africa of new realities which, spreading to infinity, will liberate new energy. These new categories, this system of unaccustomed entities, must assume the task of retranslating in detail all the excrescences with which Africa is afflicted.

In concrete terms, it will no longer do to talk of African unity; we must pursue the means. We can no longer content ourselves with abstract affirmations about African culture in general; we must elucidate scientifically what it is that makes such and such a manifestation distinctly African Negro, another Magrabin, and a third, by its origins and inspiration, strictly Arab. This is the truth, eroded sometimes by the passage of time but confirmed by cir-

---

Source: *The Black Scholar*, I, 1 (November 1969), pp. 28-30, 31-35. Reprinted by permission of the publisher.

cumstance. All of us share the desire to bridge centuries and differences and to create a united present.

It is to a review of conscience that I invite you—to a casting up of accounts, and finally to a resolution.

Since accounting there must be, I will myself speak of negritude, but I trust that all the other strains which go to make up our continent will be studied. For that is Africa.

Since we must arrive at a resolution, each one of us has a duty to regard differences in the perspective of unity.

Magrabism and Pan-Arabism are no doubt political concepts, but it would be hard to deny that their infra-structure is cultural.

Negritude thinks of itself no doubt as a purely literary concept; in truth it is today a political mysticism.

These are the problems we have earnestly to tackle.

For my part, I should like in turn, but in other terms, to take up the theme of negritude. Negritude has failed. It has failed, not in the main because a few pseudo-philosophical scribblings have attributed to it the wish to denounce a certain form of African development, but because it has become hostile to the development of Africa, denying its origins to deliver us, bound hand and foot, to ethnologists and anthropologists. The negritude we are offered is the relegation of the Negro to the slow rhythm of the fields, at the treacherous hour of neo-colonization. As Madame Kesteloot has realized a little belatedly, it is not surprising that the young no longer flock to hear her.

The approach to eternity of the negritic Negro is not a metaphysical one, but political. Negritude today fixes and coagulates for unavoidable ends the most well-worn theories about African traditions, of which it claims to be the literary expression.

By rehashing the past and tickling a morbid sensitivity, it hopes to make us forget the present. The negritude of speeches, the negritude of today provides, when the great distributions are made, the "good Negroes." Alas for the great poetic vision!

"Do you suppose," we read, "that we can beat the Europeans at mathematics, except for a few outstanding men who would confirm that we are not a race of abstractions?" This sentence was contributed by a theoretician of negritude to the UNESCO *Courier* of April 1965. Reread it; you will look in vain for poetry. What you will find is the confirmation that the zealots of negritude are not content merely to point out a difference which is, after all, understandable, but as part of this mania for upholding the concept of theoretical imperfection they endeavor consciously to oppose the black continent to a Europe which is rational and, above all, industrial.

It is easy to discern the intention behind all this intellectual confusion. From the unfinished concept of negritude one passes to another, very vague and very subtle, of the Negro soul; and thereafter to the uncertainty of a philosophy without imperatives and without foundation whose sole title is the French which, it appears, is to regenerate the world—the African world and, of course, the rest. At the end of the road we are offered African socialism which, excuse the incongruity, is merely the conclusion of a syllogism of which the premise is the lubricous Negro. This comes from no theorist of negritude, but we know our Sartre. However great our liking for him, we find passages which are mere enormities. "Negritude," he wrote,

> is not a state but an attitude, . . . an act; but an act which ignores the world, which does not tend towards transforming the wealth of the world. . . . It is a matter of existing in the midst of this world, . . . of an appropriation which is not technical.

From this it follows that for our Negro poets (and I quote):

> Existence is the repetition year by year of the sanctified coitus. . . . The human rises out of nothing like a penis in erection; creation is an immense and perpetual parturition; the world is flesh and the offspring of flesh. . . . Thus the deepest roots of negritude are androgynous.

This is sheer phantasmagoria. It is not surprising if after this the Negroes are incapable of making a revolution. Revolution is primarily technical and that is why Marx was the one to write the finest songs about the bourgeoisie.

But Sartre, in self-defense, came practically to another conclusion. It will suffice to read the final pages of that very fine text *Orphée Noir* to become aware of this. By keeping the sexual pedal pressed right down, Sartre drifted into delirium, which is normal. Negritude, by seeking fecundity elsewhere than in Africa, lapsed into socialism, which serves it right.

For we thought that African socialism derived from negritude would bring about the downfall of the oppressor's warehouses.

This idea is the winding street of revolutions and the end of all our hopes. Negritude, by pretending that socialism already existed in traditional communities and that it would be sufficient to follow African traditions to arrive at an authentic socialism, deliberately camouflaged the truth and thus became ripe for destruction.

The first outcome of all this nonsense is the ghosts which disturb our dreams at night:

> the purring of states which are running in neutral gear
> ante-diluvian demagogy
> government waltzes
> a cacophony of administrative interference in stagnant economic operations
> daily increasing cleavage between town and country
> unemployment and impotence of the educated
> lack of structural changes
> incompetent civil servants, etc.

Only frenzy and bitterness are in sight. This must change and to do this it is not sufficient to talk of negritude, for African Negroes know they are Negroes and that they are in the midst of the present African catastrophe. In other words we must deal with today's tasks.

This duty may be understood in accordance with the seriousness with which the following questions are tackled:

> How shall we modernize Africa?
> How shall we get rid of old structures?
> How shall we encourage technical culture?
> What importance should we attach to each stratum of our society?
> What place will be occupied by women and young people?
> How shall we resolve our ethnic problems?
> How shall we approach traditional religions, etc.?

For the intellectual, the worker, the shopkeeper, the peasant, and for those who do not want to travel outside the country, these are the daily problems which must be solved immediately.

Negritude, hollow, vague, and inefficient, is an ideology. There is no further place in Africa for literature other than that of the revolutionary combat. Negritude is dead.

A worrying thought arises at this point. I should like to combine this worry with my own worries. It lies in the same direction.

Doubtless, if we examine the events over the past ten years in Africa, and if we disgustedly consider this cavalcade of servility and begging, and if we measure the extent of this hypocrisy, we cannot prevent ourselves from calling for a revolt.

Africa has not gone and she does not seem to be ready for departure.

The false alarms, the courtelinesque ballets, and the tragi-comic setting of the gigantic Luna-Park make people quick to conclude that these Negroes are worth nothing and are still under the influence of their fantasies and keeping the worst surprises for the best intentions. The conclusion can be quickly drawn and it is drawn. It grieves and humiliates us and we are tempted to throw in the sponge. It could be the same for negritude.

* * *

We should consider negritude as a primitive period necessary to the African renaissance. I would say, and I choose my words carefully, that at a time when the whole world was given over to racialism and people like Andrass and Morand were taken for vagabonds, at a time when the whole of humanity raised voice in competitive cacophony, there was a single pistol-shot in the middle of this concert—negritude. It shook a few consciences and brought a few Negroes together, and this was a good thing. I do not intend to defend negritude against its internal weaknesses and the disintegration with which it is theatened.

We should nonetheless recognize that negritude's exaltation of our heroes can be none other than abstract and underlines contemporary demands. It produced poetry of the unusual and of solitude, doubtless, but at the same time that poetry was political in its refusal to betray its origins. It was political before being lyrical.

I am not speaking of deviated or perverted negritude. I am speaking of our debt, and above all, our pride, in belonging to the tradition of African civilization, and in possessing values which distinguish the black world from that of the white men. In the realm of artistic creation, this attitude calls for a casting off of European models and a profession of faith in the destiny of Africa. Formulated thus, negritude should be considered as the first moment of present-day requirements; I think that it was, yesterday, one of the possible forms for the struggle for emancipation.

It is a curious struggle, I will be told, that contents itself with words when de-personalization is rampant in Senegal and men are dying like flies in the banana fields of the West Indies. Doubtless this is so, but one should forget for an instant the negritude of the dictionary and neo-colonial imposture and should try to understand what courage was needed to dare to protest against humiliation in the "thirties." And as regards words I should recommend a little more thorough reading of Marx. One can read, in his "Contribution to the Criticism of Engels' 'Philosophy of Law,' " this phrase which may appear astonishing to some of you. I quote:

"It is evident," says Marx, "that the aim of criticism can in no wise replace criticism by armed force. Material force can only be countermanded by material force, but theory is also changed to a material force as soon as it penetrates the masses." I do not think, therefore, that the error arises at this level. The capital error of this older negritude, the great sin of negritude in general was to have been, at the outset, inverted love. It was to have believed, even before its birth, in universality—when the universe was forbidden to it. The carnal ardor of black hatred should have been opposed to the cosmic insults to which none other than the black race have been subjected. But our poets, overtaken by unreason, preferred the crazy advances of love. Damas says this when he looks in vain for "a shoulder in which to hide his face and share of reality." On behalf of us all, pigment confirms the truth that this entire negritude is morbid sterility because it never knew what harvest it would reap. And indeed, that which brings about the restructuring of the world concerns revolution, not cosmic ferment. Negritude was born dead; it was going to die and it died.

A message, however, remains. Apart from the ineffectiveness of its negation, apart from the labyrinth of mystification, negritude was a rejection of humiliation.

Today this humiliation is still apparent and the problem posed by negritude remains. There are the unwanted gifts intermittently showered upon us so as to insure our continued subjection. There is the deterioration of rates of exchange, there are the prices fixed in Paris, London, and elsewhere. And for one unemployed—let no more be said—there is the appetizing food to be had in foreign embassies. There is the isolation of China. There are the millions that foreign aid brings in to the countries that are supposed to be aiding us, and the moving text by Che Guevara:

> How can we speak of the "mutual benefits" if we have the sale, at world market prices, of raw products costing unlimited efforts and suffering to the under-developed countries and the purchase, at world market prices, of machines produced in today's great automated factories?
> If we establish this sort of relationship between the two groups of nations, we will have to agree that the Socialist countries are to a certain extent implicated in imperialist exploitation.
> It will be argued that the volume of exchanges with the under-

developed countries constitutes an insignificant percentage of Socialist countries' foreign trade. This is absolutely true, but makes no difference as to the immoral character of this exchange.

In short, there is the spirit of Camp David. And finally, there we are—divided, crushed, and pulverized. A reduced and shaken Africa, with no grasp of its future.
This is the reality set before us.
Africa, still anti-Aristotelian, is still in the expectation of form. But the great upheavals of the next decades will proceed from this unreasoning, formless Africa. All that is needed is unceasingly renewed action, an imposed discipline and, above all, a way of thinking which can embrace situations, discern difficulties, repulse determinism, and make real the new situation enabling us to reach our goal.
I would put forward the doctrine of Melanism.
One could find another name for it, but the essential thing is the cementing force and thought which, operating in the perspective of unity, reacts on particular sensibilities as do Magrabism and Arabism.

1. The Melanism which I would propose to you is open to all Nubia, i.e., Africa. It is not a new racialism but an identification. It is an affirmation of the plain fact that to be a Negro today is still to live through the violent depredations of the slave trade.

2. Melanism is the acceptance of a state of war, but with arms other than prayers and Negro spirituals. Said Machiavelli, "It is an act of humanity to take up arms in the defense of a people for whom arms are the only resource."

3. Melanism will be the unique resource of a people who can no longer decorate their torture with trophies conquered from shame. It will be, as Césaire says, the expression denying the whip. We must give the lie to negation by assigning positive tasks to each Negro.

We are not trying to racialize problems but to understand that white people have the habit of putting all Negroes into the same category and of inspiring themselves with this same common historical attack and subsequent traumatism, so as to define a strategy for the present. To put it clearly, Negroes should relegate their tears to antiquity. The battle has taken on a physical form, and should henceforth only have a physical expression.

For certain American Negroes, it would be illusory to think that the battle will end with the illusory conquest of civil rights. Even if they one day take over economic and social power, or if, in the meanwhile, they have crumbs thrown to them in the middle of hierarchies, they should know that they are nothing, so long as the Negroes of Africa have not yet completed the ascendancy, the tragedy of which was related by King Cristopher.

This all goes to say that the essential task must fall on the Negroes of Africa. And they can only carry it out by coming to agreement on the following questions:

1. Is it true that no race has been more insulted than ours?
2. Is not the present-day situation the perennialization of this humiliation?
3. Is it not true that the Africans themselves (our ancestors who acquiesced in the selling of slaves and who are the present-day apologists of modern sodomy) bear the overwhelming responsibility for this fearsome cavalcade?
4. And, as things are thus, is it worthwhile making the effect to get out of this slough of spittle, tears, and blood?
5. Finally, is there a certain and effective means of doing this? and if so, what is it?

These are five questions that Melanism would place before the conscience of each African.

For my part, I do not think much of African socialism. It is the ideological expression of a social category which installs, in a backward country, capitalism with its backward economy. It has nothing to offer us.

I therefore think that the only practical socialism is that propounded by Marx, completed by Lenin, and applied, with a greater or lesser degree of success, by the socialist countries. This socialism is the only practical possibility—with, of course, the variations imposed by geography. But we know Lenin's dictum, "Communism is the power of the Soviets plus electrification." This is not yet the case in Africa. There is also the advice given by Lenin to the 2nd Internationale. To make the great social leap forward one must, he said, have an active, organized proletariat and help from socialist governments. Now what we know of our proletariats and the present international situation condemns us to defer this hope.

There remains capitalism. I will not speak of the extent of this phenomenon, but will content myself with listing its failures by means of a quotation from Meister:

> Finally one fails to wonder about the inability of liberalism to apply to new countries the principles which made possible the spectacular development of our Western countries. By its very

development, capitalism impedes the development of new countries: the principle of the free circulation of capital empties these countries of their surpluses, while that of free enterprise kills the embryo of industrial development. To stick to these principles and leave their frontiers open means condemning these countries to the same stagnation as that reigning in Latin America, that typical product of neo-colonialism in that last century. It is obvious that the liberal way is a total failure in Africa.

Although during several decades Europe has been the theater of the greatest capitalist upheavals, and although capitalism today still appears as an extraordinarily fertile model which constantly generates free energy, here, for the African, it is, to use a metaphor, an extinguished and slag-covered volcano.

We therefore are forced to look for something else. Melanism which, I admit, is somewhat irrational, aims at keeping the sore open and, by shelving the solutions so far proposed, gets rid of the inextricable estrangement and founds the state in which the future history of Africa will take on a meaning.

I have already defined Melanism. It is not just a phobia. As it cannot be compared to the "anti-racist racism" Sartre speaks of in *Orphée Noire*, it is our purpose here to de-mystify the concept of race and to wrench it out of the hands of reactionary politicians who are using it to obscure the issue.

Although Sartre's objective was the same as ours—to denounce the evil that has led to the racism of the black poets—ours differs from his in that it does not limit itself to exorcising race by making it active, but aims at strengthening a people by a racial awareness, a people which perhaps is still abstract although not paradoxical, and which is probably mistaken as a result of inhibition.

There remains however, in spite of the precautions taken, something which should not be left obscure. We should repeat here what we have already said:

1. We are products of white unreason: we are Negroes only for the whites. In Africa, to be a Negro, is to be as natural as the infinite stars in the night.

2. Whatever our opinions, whether we are Christians, Muslims, Communists, or reactionaries, and often at the height of battle, white necessity has been burnt to a cinder in our flesh.

3. As it is our purpose to save ourselves from racism by constructing a modern state in Africa, this our purpose can only be made real

by an exacerbated nationalism, the force of which, although partly deriving from objective facts, also derives, according to Renouvin, from irrational elements. Consequently, we cannot reject the irrational part of such an enterprise. On the contrary, if we take the end into account, the objective pursued will give the enterprise a positive value, as has always been the case throughout history. Undoubtedly, to be able to speak of national feeling, we should, according to the well-known pattern, first have a nation. But who could deny that Islam has favored nationalism? And is it possible, as Renouvin asks, to understand anything about Japanese nationalism without referring to Shintoism?

Our project therefore, far from floundering through imaginative excesses, may break silence in pointing to the beyond and in rejecting limits. It states the necessity for a modern state while indicating the means to attain it.

Therefore it takes its inspiration from the great nationalist upsurges of past centuries, but with the difference that, although it may serve to create a myth, this myth should draw its truth only from its own strength: we need a myth which is not mythical but a reality shattered in the bric-a-brac of time. A myth such as the one Gramsci, who pronounced the only right and profound judgment on Machiavelli, discovered in *The Prince,* which he considered as an "illustration of political ideology which does not present itself as a frigid Utopia or a doctrinaire argument, but as the creation of a concrete reasoning process which operates on a dispersed and scattered people to provoke and organize their collective renaissance."

In the same way, Africa must be convinced by meditation on race. It should come to terms with its present so as to regenerate the future. In this connection, there are two objectives:

The establishment of a collective melanian will.
New mental structures.

There are five prerequisites for attaining these objectives:
1. On the political level: the establishment of a modern state.
2. On the economical level: a democratic national economy.
3. In the field of the philosophy of history, rejection of all systems which persist in discovering cyclic returns and deny indefinite progress.
4. On the intellectual and moral level: (a) in the moral field, an educational system drawing its force from a constant reference to past and present humiliations of the race and which also considers reprehensible any insane cult of the past, even borrowings from

abroad. (b) in the intellectual field, opposition to stifled traditions, an appeal for rational innovations of the various world revolutions.

5. Lastly, on the level of personal training, we should only strive for a perpetual creation of ourselves by ourselves and for a constant creative activity based upon a sense of initiative and responsibility and only retaining elements useful for the nation.

To sum up, pending the union of the whole of Africa, this transitional ideology aims at the establishment of a strong and prosperous national state which:

> Inside the country brings about the recovery of the race by vivisection!
> Outside the country asserts Africa irredentism using subversion if necessary;
> Finally, on the economic level, takes advantage of the contradictions between and inside the power coalitions in order to found a modern industry and economy.

A hallucination? Perhaps. In any case, the present methods will have to be transformed. Practical and theoretical necessities often entail the introduction of new concepts into the problem.

Before socialist recovery, must come recovery of ourselves. This is not a matter of repudiation. Tactics had to be changed. We are changing them.

In any case, these ideas are directed to the young Africans of my generation, to the generation which, like me, will perhaps not see the promised land, but which should know that the shore exists. Melanism is, after all, the preliminary to socialism. Instead of disdain and condescension, each African, as is more or less the case with the Chinese today, will read in the eyes of the European the first signs of terror.

MARTIN L. KILSON, JR.

Kilson is a professor of government at Harvard University and a student of African affairs. He has published extensively in periodicals and is the author of *Political Change in a West African State: A Study of the Modernization Process in Sierra Leone* (1966). He has edited with Rupert Emerson an anthology entitled *The Political Awakening of Africa* (1965).

The critical comments he made about blackness were offered as part of a symposium which Yale University sponsored in 1969 to help in the formulation of a black studies program at the university.

Martin L. Kilson, Jr.

The Intellectual Validity of Studying the Black Experience

Mary McCarthy, the novelist and superb and eloquent critic of the grotesque Vietnam war, remarked in the *New York Review of Books* not long ago that, whatever intellectuals do with their skills and their cleverness, they should never shirk doing what they do best—namely, to "smell a rat" and to dissect its nature and character, letting the chips fall where they may. Now, to some extent in my brief remarks on the intellectual validity of the black experience this is what I shall attempt to do: to smell a rat. I think the best approach in addressing this topic is to assess conceptually what the black experience has been and has meant. Such assessment, I think, is not easy at all. For one thing, what contemporaneous yardstick does one use to define the historical limits, the starting point, and the context of the black experience? How do we decide what is meaningful and valuable in the social, cultural, and political realities of the black experience? Furthermore, what community or segment of that vast group of people known as black people should be used as typifying whatever the black experience is and has been? For example, should we use as typical the Republic of Haiti where black men have ruled a sovereign state since the nineteenth century? But where, also, such black rule—or, if you prefer, black power—has been oppressive and dysfunctional for the black masses or lower classes? Or, perhaps, should we take the present-day state of Nigeria, where the polity is rent asunder by fratricidal warfare that was sparked by a grotesque genocidal act committed by one segment against another in this largest of all black communities in the world? Or, perhaps, should we take as typical of this thing, "the black experience," the Afro-

Source: Robinson, Foster, and Ogilvie, eds., *Black Studies in the University: A Symposium* (New Haven: Yale University Press, 1969), pp. 13–16. Copyright © 1969 by Yale University. Reprinted by permission.

American community which was subjected to chattel slavery for over two hundred years and in the past century has been denied the elemental attributes of modern citizenship and humanity by devious, grotesque, and brutal forms of white racism?

For some Negroes, particularly those imbued with an intense black racialist outlook, the answer to these perplexing questions is, unfortunately, rather easy and self-evident. From this vantage point, white police brutality against blacks in Harlem or Mississippi or South Africa or Rhodesia should constitute the contemporaneous yardstick for the historical delimitation of the black experience. With this yardstick, therefore, it would be unthinkable, if not treasonable, to use the Haitian political experience as a historical example of something relevant and meaningful to the overall black experience. Instead, one would have to select a historical event like the slave trade to the Western Hemisphere in order to find the ideological, emotional, and therapeutic sustenance for what I call the black racialist or black nationalist view of the black experience. In this view of the black experience, the slave trade is seen as the beastly act of beastly white men, or, in Malcolm X's memorable phrase, "white devils," who without pity or remorse wrenched millions of Negro Africans from their ancestral homeland for enforced and dehumanizing labor in the plantations of the Western Hemisphere. Moreover, this horrendous historical act by "white devils" has, in the black racialist view of the black experience, endowed the black man with a special aura of righteousness—indeed that same righteousness that has been applied to the oppressed and wretched of the earth ever since the birth of Christianity.

Now, of course, the typical black nationalist would not today attribute to Christian doctrine his view of the special aura of righteousness accruing to the oppressed and despised black man. Yet, it is certainly one of the striking ironies of the black nationalist approach to the black experience that the Christian doctrine, now considered a historical agent of the black man's degradation, actually informs the notion of righteousness now considered a special preserve of the black man and the black experience. In this connection, it can be remarked that all men, black and white, yellow and red, choose those historical paradoxes or ironies found suitable or useful for a given occasion and reject those lacking such utility. In this respect, therefore, the black experience is, I dare say, little more than an offshoot of the human experience—no better and no worse.

Perhaps I could put this point in sharper relief by reference to other features of the slave trade to the Western Hemisphere that seldom appear in the black nationalist's view of this horrifying historical event. To those who take the historiography of the slave trade seriously, as I do myself, it is commonplace knowledge that leading and entrepreneurial groups in traditional Negro African societies were voluntarily privy to the slave trade. These groups saw the trade in slaves as an economic relationship from which enormous wealth, profit, and political and military advantage could be derived. When such gain is available, men, I submit, will seek it. They are not likely to let cultural or racial or other bonds stand in the way. What is more, the African brokers in the slave trade—of whom there were literally tens of thousands—were not restrained by knowledge that perhaps 40 percent of the human cargo in Middle Passage perished before reaching the plantations of the Western Hemisphere. In short, I would suggest most firmly that the black experience is truly nothing more than a variant of the human experience. Put another way, and rather cynically, power is what power does.

I trust that what I have been trying to say illuminates some aspects of the intellectual validity of the black experience. I have purposely refrained from defining specifically what I mean by "the intellectual validity of the black experience." I happen to hate definitions. I have also consciously refrained from attempting to deduce a conception of the validity of the black experience as exemplified in the past three centuries of black-white relationships.

I am, I think, reasonably knowledgeable about the bloody and dehumanizing record of this relationship; but I consider it neither unique nor a startling event. All men are capable of it and, indeed, all men, black and white, yellow and red, have been privy to such. Moreover, I cannot quite accept the viewpoint that the black man's experience with white oppression has endowed black men with a special insight into oppression and thus a special capacity to rid human affairs of oppression. I would argue, in fact, that this viewpoint is largely a political one which certain groups find serviceable in the contemporary conflict between Negro and white in American society. Indeed, it is a common fallacy to believe that what is momentarily politically serviceable is *ipso facto* intellectually virtuous. I personally understand this viewpoint as held by black nationalists. Indeed, I am compassionate toward it. But my intellect rejects it. Like Mary McCarthy, I begin to smell a rat and feel compelled to dissect it for all to see.

ERNIE MKALIMOTO

Ernie Mkalimoto is a central staff member of the *League of Revolutionary Black Workers* in Detroit. He was previously co-director of education and culture for *Black Mind* in Harlem, and is currently a member of the editorial board of the *Journal of Black Poetry*. He has written a number of essays and poems which, along with translations, have appeared in black journals.

In this essay he offers a forceful interpretation of the cultural aspects of black nationalism which most effectively sums up the position taken by many of the more radical black thinkers and ideologues in contemporary America.

Ernie Mkalimoto

Revolutionary Black Culture: The Cultural Arm of Revolutionary Nationalism

Gentle rain of dark consciousness upon the Mother-Earth/new dawn singing in a bobbing sea of cocoahearts/sway of ebony breasts cradling the nation in spirit-fires of black rebirth/dark warriors take their place upon the soil, our soil, bearing chants of the dead who are not dead: Chaka, Vesey, Toussaint, Garvey, Malcolm . . . New energies released upon eroded, stale rhythms of the planet/trembling earth/burning sky/SUNRISE! Exploding in the rainbows of a new dawn, of spiritual rebirth, chanting the Word as it sows the seeds of the new Man who has come to claim his earth again, to claim his right to govern again, to claim his will to live again, this is Black Nationalism, the political, economic, and cultural expression of the black, colonized nation of North America.

But what is Black Nationalism? In its most general terms, Black Nationalism may be defined as the *feeling* among African-Americans that their destiny is a common one, that whatever affects one black person ultimately affects all black people. This feeling—by definition a subjective phenomenon—is rooted within the objective, historical factor of a common racial oppression which black people have undergone within the United States, a process which began in slavery and which has continued up to the present day. And it is out of the jagged world of racial oppression that Black Nationalism has flowed into being: strongly evident at times, such as during the era of the pre-Civil War nationalist movement in the North, the Garvey movement, and the present historical period; at other times more covert, such as during the period of Reconstruction, as well as the abortive integration plunge into "the mainstream" fostered by the educated black middle class following World War II.

Source: *Negro Digest*, XIX, 2 (December 1969), pp. 11–17. Reprinted by permission of *Negro Digest* and Ernie Mkalimoto. Copyright © December 1969 by Ernie Mkalimoto.

On the other hand, what is black culture? If culture in its most general terms may be defined as the *way of life* of a people, the reflection in the minds and manners of men of the politics and economics of their given society, black culture, then, is the way of life of black people, the life-style of African-Americans who have been forced to live under the oppressive politics and economics (as well as culture) of a domestic colonialism within the United States. And here it is essential to distinguish between culture in general, which is life-style, and the artistic and literary works which constitute the embodiment—some would say refinement—of this culture (these works constituting only a small portion of the totality; for black culture is not only Pharoah Sanders overstepping the bounds of western consciousness in his probings of Karma, or the revolutionary poet, Askia Muhammad Touré, rapping from the vibrant heights of Harlem's Black Mind; or even Leon Thomas doing some down, black yodeling to the African rhythm of bells at the foot of Mt. Morris park; but black culture is also the thunder of maroon pants, orange dashikis, and green alligators splashing out of hot, swirling summer clouds of Lenox Avenue blues people, is black talk and C. P.-time, is black life-style, is Christian heritage, is the way in which black people live/hope to live. And as culture is the expression of national consciousness (Fanon), the vehicle par excellence by which the life-forces of the nation are canalized, it is impossible to speak of Black Nationalism without considering at the same time the question of black culture; *culture and nationalism cannot be separated.* And this is why one must be extremely careful in the use of the term, "cultural nationalism," an expression which almost takes on the appearance of redundancy, and which today has been programmed by certain obfuscators of the struggle to mean almost anything from "traitor" to "racist." But then, what is "cultural nationalism"? To answer this question necessitates a return to our preliminary remarks.

CULTURAL NATIONALISM

All nationalism begins with feeling, a common sentiment which is anchored within certain objective factors (a common oppression, history, language, territory, etc.). From the social foundation concretized in this unity of feeling arises the edifice of nationalist *ideology* (representing a step forward from the relatively "primitive" stage of folklore and stereotypes; the first stirrings of national consciousness); like any other ideology it may be passed through the political spectrometer where it separates into its three fundamental components:

politics, economics, and culture. The cultural component of nationalism rests upon two pillars:
1. The development of a *system* of national values and mores.
2. The development of a national history.

Through emphasis upon the particular life-style and historic achievements of the nation's people (and, by projection, of the achievements to come), a sense of national pride, of patriotism, is instilled in the hearts of the people, resulting in a fusion of human energy forces which, depending upon which national class is leading the struggle (or heading the government, whatever the case), may take on a variety of political directions; in the case where culture is allowed to prevail over politics (*bourgeois*-oriented leadership) this phenomenon is known as "cultural nationalism."

"Cultural nationalism," then, is the expression of the struggle to promote/sustain a particular way of life, a devotion to that way of life within the national community, but a struggle either divorced from politics, or one in which so-called cultural imperatives are allowed to dominate political necessities. Manifesting itself for the most part within the confines of small sects or cults having no tangible relation to the masses of the black nation, this form of nationalism may perhaps pretend to its reflecting the totality of black culture, but in reality that would be false, for it apparently does not consider the revolutionary struggle of African-Americans as being worthy of inclusion within the black cultural dynamic. Not that "cultural nationalism" in every case closes its eyes to the realities of the present, but when it finally does address itself to the question of white oppression, it does so many times under the guise of a terminological confusion out of which it can justify, at least on the surface, its unwillingness to meet imperialism on a toe-to-toe, no-holds-barred, revolutionary, political terrain.

Here the oppression of African-Americans is defined as "cultural": the imposition of an alien way of life upon black people. From a cultural problem must emerge a cultural solution, the creation of a new way of life in contradistinction to the old. But divorced from politics this stance is rendered absolutely meaningless, for the suppression of the original black cultures in North America was not carried out primarily through either the verbal or written negation of its existence by the colonizer—that would come later. The suppression of black language, black religion, black names, black vestment, and the black family—in short, black life-style—was enacted by *political* means, by the pale fist of white state power wielded against the black collectivity by the slavemaster. And so today, even though it is the arm of a cultural imperialism which constantly attempts to distort and destroy the foundations of an independent black lifestyle within this alien land, this encroachment is only possible because of the political power of the white state which lends teeth to the cultural jaws of our political oppression here on this continent. Our collective problem is, at base, no more a "cultural" than a "moral" one.

REVOLUTIONARY NATIONALISM

On the other hand, in the case where politics evolves into a *revolutionary* struggle for control of the state (the seizure of state power), when the leadership is one which represents the broad masses of the nation, then the parallel struggle waged on the cultural front for the purpose of supporting national revolutionary politics is no longer the strictured enigma of "cultural nationalism," but the assertion of *revolutionary culture,* the cultural arm of Revolutionary Nationalism in which politics assumes the leading role. This is the point where culture links itself with the day-to-day aspirations of the people, guiding these collective energies to the crystallizing point of revolution and laying a new basis of values for the emerging society. In this sense, the struggle along cultural lines cannot be considered simply as a catalyst for Revolutionary Nationalism, and then once having fulfilled this role losing its *raison d'être* and falling to the wayside of history; for revolutionary black culture, the new system of black values and mores reflected in the politics and economics of the black communal society to be born in the flames of revolutionary struggle, not only primes the struggle for national liberation, but is the aim of this struggle as well: a way of life which will restore the harmonious relationship of Man to himself and to other men, of Man to the changing forces of Nature. To this end, revolutionary black culture, the cultural arm of Revolutionary Black Nationalism, must unite black people, must arouse the collective consciousness of the black nation and pose an alternative to the moribund, decadent culture of the oppressor, challenging every move it makes on black terrain. And perhaps most important of all, revolutionary black culture must reveal to African-Americans the way in which their oppression must be brought to an end. Otherwise the question would no longer remain one of culture, but of pure and simple mystification.

All nationalisms have had recourse to the development of a national history, to an unearthing of treasured historic facts buried deep within the nation's past, for it is only through the projection and study of this history that a *solidarity in time* (Césaire) is provided for the nation, that those bobbing leaves reflected in the gropings of the present can ultimately be joined to the stable roots of the past, lending anchor to the national base. For the African on the mother continent as well as abroad this development (or rather, redevelopment) of national histories is of crucial necessity in light of the *historic discontinuities* which were savagely introduced within our life-styles by the colonizing West. And the historic discontinuity present within our culture today is not only that which separates the experiences of the present generation of black militants from those of the "twenties" and "thirties" (Cruse), but in a much more general sense that which separates the entire captive black nation from its history here on this continent, as well as the knowledge of the leading role which our ancestors played in Africa as molders and shapers of human civilization upon the planet.

Black history must continue to be resurrected on these two fronts and taken to the people. But in doing so, Revolutionary Black Nationalism submits that knowledge of the past can in no way change the material conditions of the present; only that this knowledge can enable black people to more effectively deal with the present (instead of vice versa), to redevelop the sense of collective self, and to avoid the dangers of known pitfalls characteristic to struggles of national liberation. And in contrast to certain forms of "cultural nationalism" which wallow in the insanity of fantastically concocted mythologies, in the exchange of black irrationality for white irrationality, Revolutionary Nationalism holds that in the further development of our national history—though in part a reaction to the sterile myth perpetrated by the technological barbarians of the West that the black man never invented anything, never created any great civilizations, never possessed a written language, indeed, never had a history—we have no need of producing a counter-myth which only ends in the further confusion of our people. Our history stands on its own merits, and has no need of escapist fantasies which warp black psyches. . . .

MISGUIDED CRITICISMS OF BLACK CULTURE

There exists a justifiable basis upon which "cultural nationalism" can be criticized, then, once one is brought to a face-to-face understanding of the only really valid meaning of the term. But the recent assaults upon this singularly popular scapegoat from the "psychotic fringe" of the struggle are only harbingers of more ominous forces which see in nationalism the fundamental threat to black people determining their own destiny on the American continent; like the case of the blind men examining the elephant, the extremities of nationalism are taken for the entire phenomenon, and consequently these attacks can be given either one of two interpretations: either the negro "revolutionary" possesses a total ignorance of the role of the cultural within the revolutionary process, or he understands too well, and in either case these attacks can mean nothing more than a *deliberate, systematic attempt* to destroy the cultural dynamic of black nationalism, and, since there can be no question of separating culture from nationalism, *they constitute an attempt to destroy black nationalism per se,* all in the sacrosanct and therefore apparently unchallengeable name of "the revolution."

Unfortunately, the present trend in this direction dictates that one will see in the coming months an attempt by sandal-lickers of the "Negro revolution" to associate more and more the question of black nationalism with that of "black racism," an obvious parroting of the ideology of the white power structure (take note). And when these attacks upon "cultural nationalism" heave from the ramparts of slick, white-controlled "leftist" magazines (of ambiguous financial backing), then the circle is fully drawn, and one begins to understand clearly the implications: the "revolution" to which our confused militants aspire will revolve around a *white,* western-oriented cultural matrix. . . .

What is the significance? It is a phenomenon which reveals in no uncertain terms that the concept of revolution in the minds of our "new breed" of leaders does not mean a return to the best of the ancient values and practices left to us by our ancestors, but is instead reduced to nothing more than a synonym for turning white–*integration,* if you will, but this time with "guns and force" in lieu of picket signs and pray-ins. Thus, what began originally as a desire to whiten the struggle (and thereby become white) has today evolved into the form (and only form) of an intense "ideological" debate in which the question of coalitions with whites—already resolved in practice during the 1930's and again within the brief period of Civil Rights struggle during the early 1960's—are rehashed and chewed again like stale vomit for the benefit of none and the confusion of all. For behind the veil of revolutionary rhetoric, of hysterical cries of "class struggle," and of united fronts against a fascism which does not yet exist lies—and this must be said—a basic hate of self and kind, with "politics" used merely as the legitimizing factor.

White; therefore non-black; therefore alienation, that is to say, alien to our nation; therefore a revolution plagued with abortion even *before* its conception. For if revolution means struggle on the politico/military front, it means no less a struggle on the ideological/cultural front. And if a given revolution finds itself bathed in the light of brilliant military successes, it is nonetheless true that this very same revolution can discover its political gains *reversed* if proper attention is not paid to work in the ideological/cultural areas.[1]

For a revolution which disparages or ignores the cultural domain will see this vacuum which it has neglected filled from the eroded ladle of the *dominant* culture, that is to say the culture of the *dominant class or nation* (in this case, white America), and if it is in the name of a new way of life that we are willing to shed the last of our blood and expel our last, wavering breath, our neglect of the cultural aspects of our revolution would lead to the early demise of our newborn nation-state and a return to the value system of the old.

Our cause, then, is not to struggle against black culture, but against the mystification and misuse of that culture (which only increases and perpetuates the psychology of escapism inherent in the life-styles of black Americans), not against those of our artists and cultural leaders who are attempting to revolutionize within the domain of the cultural universe, but against those ever-present armies of parasites upon the struggle who would have us play political "ostrich" in a world where the dodo bird has already become quite extinct. For though the gun is without a doubt a primary weapon in any revolutionary struggle, we should constantly remind ourselves that it is not the *only* form of struggle, nor is it by any means the only *necessary* form. Black poets, actors, writers, and artists, as well as political and military cadres, must *all* join hands with the masses of our people in one common effort—"different strokes for different folks," certainly, but all swimming in the same general direction: *black people governing themselves again*. Planet power to the peoples of color. We will win!

[1] Witness the intensity of struggle along these lines within the Chinese Cultural Revolution: the struggle waged by the Chinese in order to keep their revolution from straying along the path of bourgeoisification, or in terms used by the Chinese, of the "restoration of capitalism."

Annotated Bibliography

Annotated Bibliography

While there are still too few critical studies devoted to the tricontinental aspects of the ideology of blackness, a number of valuable monographs concerned with regional developments do exist. Among those works offering a broad scope, the reader is directed to the following: Janheinz Jahn, *Neo-African Literature: A History of Black Writing* (New York: Grove Press, 1969); and Mercer Cook and Stephen E. Henderson, *The Militant Black Writer in Africa and the United States* (Madison: University of Wisconsin Press, 1969). The former is something of a compendium with brief analyses of the most important writers and the "schools" to which they belong. It serves both as a good introduction and a useful reference work. The latter is the published version of two lectures, each separately directed to the development of African and American black consciousness, but jointly forming a very readable and informative introductory essay. "Negro Creativity: The Writer," an issue of *African Forum* (I, 4, 1966), offers a number of contemporary perspectives by outstanding figures like Léopold Senghor and Langston Hughes. George Shepperson, "Notes on Negro-American Influences on the Emergence of African Nationalism" (*Journal of African History*, I, 2, 1960, pp. 299–312) is a most significant seminal work in which the author effectively demonstrates the role black American writings had on the formation of modern African thought.

An intelligent appreciation of the significance of the African past on contemporary black American thought can be obtained through a reading of the essays in *African Seen by American Negroes* (Paris: Présence Africaine, 1958), and *The American Negro Writer and His Roots* (New York: American Society for African Culture, 1960). E. U. Essiem-Udom treats another phase of this development in his "The Relationship of Afro-Americans to African Nationalism" (*Freedomways*, II, 4, 1962, pp. 391–407). Certainly mention should be made of the investigations undertaken by Melville Herskovits into the subject of black cultural exchange, such as in the posthumous collections of essays, *The New World Negro* (Bloomington: Indiana University

Press, 1966), and most notably in Section V of that volume, entitled "The Arts."

Many interesting studies dealing with the emergence of modern African culture and literature, particularly the search for African identity, are now available. Robert July, *The Origins of Modern African Thought* (New York: Frederick A. Praeger, Inc., 1967) is a successful attempt to pattern West African thought and to relate its development to a growing opposition toward European colonialism. More directly concerned with literary themes, and providing one of the best brief assessments of negritude available in English, is Claude Wauthier, *The Literature and Thought of Modern Africa* (New York: Frederick A. Praeger, Inc., 1967). A most sympathetic and insightful interpretation of the literary aspects of negritude is Thomas Melone's *De la negritude dans la littérature negro-africaine* (Paris: Présence Africaine, 1962). But the fullest treatment of negritude and of its historical development is given by Lilyan Kesteloot, *Les Écrivains noirs de langue française: Naissance d'une littérature* (Brussels: Université libre de Bruxelles, 1963). Complements to the work of Melone and Kesteloot are the two more politically oriented essays written by Abiola Irele, "Negritude or Black Cultural Nationalism" (*Journal of Modern African Studies*, III, 3, 1965, pp. 321–346), and "Negritude —Literature and Ideology" (*Journal of Modern African Studies*, III, 4, 1965, pp. 499–526).

Too little is readily available on the Caribbean aspects of black cultural development. G. R. Coulthard, *Race and Colour in Caribbean Literature* (London: Oxford University Press, 1962) is a good general introduction. On Haiti, one would find profitable Naomi M. Garrett, *The Renaissance of Haitian Poetry* (Paris: Présence Africaine, 1963), and *Haiti: Poètes Noirs* (Paris: Éditions du Seuil for Présence Africaine, 1951).

The black American writer has been the subject of a wide variety of recent critical studies. Perhaps the best known—and frequently criticized—is Harold Cruse, *The Crisis of the Negro Intellectual* (New York: William Morrow and Company, Inc., 1967) which is not only an analytical survey but also offers interesting evaluations of the Harlem renaissance and of West Indian influences on black American literature and culture in the 1920's. Alain Locke, *The New Negro: An Interpretation*, published in 1925 (New York: Johnson Reprint Corporation, 1968), is a classic in its own right and provides a still-valuable interpretation of black culture in the 1920's. LeRoi Jones, *Blues People: Negro Music in White America* (New York: William Morrow and Company, Inc., 1963) contains some very insightful commentary on the black cultural situation in white America. For an evaluation of the different types of contemporary thought about black politics and culture, see Solomon P. Gethers, "Black Power: Three Years Later" (*Negro Digest,* XIX, 2, 1969, pp. 4–10, 69–81). Among the most recent studies produced is that of Theodore Draper, *The Rediscovery of Black Nationalism* (New York: The Viking Press, Inc., 1970). Integrationist in interpretation, this work, while carefully studied and written, is lacking in an appreciation of the positive aspects of black nationalism.

Finally, the reader should turn to the lively periodical literature in which some of the best contemporary interpretations of the ideology of blackness are to be found. *Présence africaine,* official organ of the Society of African Culture and standard bearer of the idea of negritude, was founded in 1947 and has offered critical essays, fiction, and poetry by the best writers of French-speaking Africa, among whom are Senghor, Camara Laye, and David Diop. (It has also printed articles by blacks from the Caribbean and the United States, including Frantz Fanon, Aimé Césaire, Langston Hughes, and W. E. B. Du Bois.) Inspired by the Society of African Culture, a group of black Americans created the American Society of African Culture, which published, all too briefly, a first-rate journal of interpretation, *African Forum.* In recent years, a number of well-edited black journals of opinion have appeared. The two most meriting attention and indicating the direction of contemporary politically advanced black thought are *Freedomways* and *The Black Scholar. Black World,* formerly *The Negro Digest,* has been a vehicle for new black fiction for some time and has also published some fine critical interpretations of the contemporary black mood.

One bibliography is particularly worth mentioning to the introductory student: Janheinz Jahn, *Bibliography of Neo-African Literature from Africa, America, and the Caribbean* (New York: Frederick A. Praeger, Inc., 1965).